FOOD AND DRINK

BOOK 3

THE Food & Drink BOOK 3

Michael Barry
Jill Goolden
Chris Kelly

BBC BOOKS

Illustrations: Colin Hadley
Photographs: Sara Taylor
Stylist: Tessa Rosier
Home economist: Mary Cadogan

Published by BBC Books
A division of BBC Enterprises Limited
Woodlands, 80 Wood Lane
London W12 0TT

First published 1987
© Michael Barry, Jill Goolden, Chris Kelly 1987

ISBN 0 563 20609 8

Colour printing by Chorley and Pickersgill, Leeds
Photoset and printed in Great Britain by
Redwood Burn Limited, Trowbridge, Wiltshire

ACKNOWLEDGEMENTS

Food and Drink would like to thank the following for their help in the preparation of this book:

Joan Morgan
Peter Dodd
John Masson
Sandy Ross
Ken Clements
Patrick Holden
Sue Hill
Donald Cooper
Mr & Mrs Henry Stockdale
Peter Murrin
Michael Smith
Prue Leith
Germaine Greer
Jonathan Bedford
Donald Mackinlay
Daphne Metland.

CONTENTS

INTRODUCTION

In the middle of January 1987, when Britain was suffering one of the coldest spells this century, Michael Barry suggested we do an oxtail casserole on *Food and Drink*. He calculated its rich, heart-warming properties would appeal to a shivering nation. Once liberated from the frozen wastelands of mid-Kent (at one point – quite seriously – it looked as though a helicopter would be the only way) he duly demonstrated the recipe on the programme.

One of the advantages of live broadcasting is that we could take such decisions the day before, or even on the day. Michael – as he often does – struck a resounding chord with his casserole. But the poor, unsuspecting butchers were not amused. The morning after, queues formed outside their shops and there were no oxtails to be had within three days. Some butchers even instituted waiting lists. It was all somewhat reminiscent of wartime rationing – no doubt some latter-day Cpl. Joneses were dispensing oxtails under the counter to favoured customers.

In this third *Food and Drink* book you'll find the oxtail recipe amongst many others of Michael Barry's, along with buying and eating advice from Chris Kelly and highly practical information about a whole range of drinks from Jill Goolden. What are the lessons of the oxtail saga? Well, not just that Michael's recipes are hugely popular, though that is true. The real lessons are that millions of us care very much about what we eat, we want new recipe ideas and we welcome being reminded of traditional favourites which may have been forgotten since the onslaught of processed and convenience foods. We who make *Food and Drink* are privileged to have a weekly audience of five to six million people who take such an *active* interest in the subject. When a task force of that size votes with its shopping bags, the food industry has to take note. And a good thing, too. Whatever excuses the butchers may have expressed (mostly in purple prose to my office), many simply didn't bother to stock oxtail any more. Next winter we hope they will, and they certainly will if we all continue to cook recipes such as oxtail casserole.

It is a marvellous time to be writing and broadcasting about food and drink: the nation's diet – quite rightly – has become a political issue; more and more people are anxious to have a healthier diet; at last, eating out is becoming a major leisure activity; generations reared on processed food are returning to the pleasures of home cooking; food retailers vie with each other to offer the greatest choice and quality – indeed, there's a growing understanding of, and demand for, quality; appreciation of wines is no longer confined to stately homes; 'ethnic' cuisines are now popular not only in restaurants but also at home. I make no apologies for setting down a list of this sort – I have merely noted *some* of the developments that make food and drink such invigorating subjects at the moment. I am sure Michael Barry, Chris Kelly and Jill Goolden attribute the success of their previous two books as well as that of the programme (the most popular food series ever on BBC 2) in part to the climate in which they operate.

This third book offers the same rich choice of practical advice garnished with a certain amount of humour, proving food and drink can really be about *enjoyment*. Chris Kelly has written introductions to each chapter, Michael Barry provides the recipes with tips and Jill Goolden contributes a wealth of down-to-earth advice on everything from whisky and wine to water.

Now, a word or two about this triumvirate of authors. Michael Barry's first job in television was shifting scenery for *Emergency Ward Ten*. From such an auspicious beginning he became, in turns, a radio drama producer, a *Radio Newsreel* reporter and then a television producer in BBC Current Affairs. Wearing that hat he worked on such flagship programmes as *Tonight* and *24 Hours*. There was, however, another influence at work, though as yet not apparent. Michael's mother taught home economics and from a very early age he had developed not only great enthusiasm for cooking, but also a sound knowledge of the skills and techniques involved.

In the early seventies, Michael's broadcasting and culinary activities met. He was the first programme controller at London's Capital Radio, and he had placed a regular cookery spot in Michael Aspel's morning programme. When the normal presenter was unavailable Michael Barry had a go and The Crafty Cook was born. The reaction of Capital's listeners was very much the same as *Food and Drink*'s – his own brand of enthusiasm, blended in equal measures with simplicity, craftiness and catholicism, proved immensely popular. The reactions are not always predictable, though. During the last series I received a letter from lecturers at a Welsh polytechnic, who were teaching English to the wives of Japanese businessmen working for Honda. The lecturers told me they used video recordings of Michael's recipes to aid them in their task. This conjured up an extraordinary prospect for us – Michael's use of his own personal language when demonstrating recipes had long been a private joke ('gunge', 'splodge', 'whirr' and so on). Were these Japanese ladies now conversing with the uncomprehending Welsh in Michael Barry's personal onomatopoeic language? Well, perhaps I can perform a small service for all concerned by providing a modest glossary of words Michael actually used during the last series.

BLODGET: the act of placing the filling in a mince pie
BLONK: the repetitive noise of a cooking process (as in 'blonk, blonk, blonk')
GLOPPY: from 'gloppiness' – the consistency of a cake batter when it reaches the desired thickness
GRUNCH: to grind
GRUNGING: scholars dispute the precise definition but this is thought to be the action of a pestle in a mortar
ZUZ: to mix ingredients in a food processor

In this collection of Michael Barry's recipes we have persuaded him to curb some of his more extreme linguistic habits. Divided into six sections are a selection of his best recipes, some culled from the last series and some appearing for the first time. From excellent ideas for smoked fish to delicious vegetarian dishes, from the secrets of perfect roast beef to a wonderful game pie, from some exciting ethnic recipes to some wickedly self-indulgent puddings ... all are easy to follow and straightforward to prepare. That is the essence of Michael's 'crafty cooking'.

Jill Goolden started her professional life as a magazine sub-editor. The first published article she remembers was a leader for *The Field* about showjumping. She was also responsible for padding out the correspondence page if there were not enough readers' letters. She duly wrote to herself on a number of occasions, inventing a certain 'Z. Dobson', who allegedly lived at the unlikely address of Beeswing, Kirkcudbrightshire. She even managed to generate a 'reader's' poem on the glories of Wales by passing a piece of paper around the sub-editors' desk and getting everyone to contribute one line. It was apparently a great success.

Jill has since written in her own right on everything from sexual harassment to marriage (not that one leads to the other). She has worked at *Vogue* and the *Daily Telegraph*, amongst others. Another staff position was on *Brides* magazine, a very significant job as it turns out. The editor asked Jill to commission an article about champagne. Jill then commissioned *herself* (rather than the mysterious Miss Dobson), and a career in wine journalism began. Since then she has contributed to most national magazines and newspapers on the subject, as well as broadcasting on radio and television.

Jill selected herself for *Food and Drink*, having appeared in a previous version of the series. More than anyone else I can think of, she really understands the revolution in drinking habits that has been taking place in the eighties. Millions more are buying wine than ever before, but they are buying from supermarkets and spending less than £3 a bottle. What the consumers desperately seek – and what Jill gives in abundance – is simple advice and straightforward recommendations. Most wine writers still dispense somewhat more sophisticated advice to a much narrower audience. Vive la différence!

In the past few years Jill has extended her repertoire considerably and this book is evidence of her wider range. As well as introducing us to two invaluable buying guides for red and white wines, and giving us sound advice on how to match wine with food, she also writes about sherries, whiskies, waters and fruit juice. Ah, you didn't realise there was much to be said about water and fruit juice? Read her chapters and you will discover there is as much to be written about quality and value-for-money on these topics as on any others.

Chris Kelly was a well known and well respected broadcaster and journalist long before he was lured into the *Food and Drink* studio. He was for many years a narrator on Granada's *World in Action*, and a producer for the same company. He has presented a whole range of radio and television programmes on a variety of subjects, in particular, about the cinema. More recently, however, he has become a television thriller writer – the work will be revealed shortly and I am on pain of death to give no inkling of the plot.

When I first discussed with Chris the possibility of presenting *Food and Drink* I did not know that many of his antecedents had actually been involved in the food industry, and they included a farmer, a baker and an hotelier. In fact, the oft-quoted legend in one part of the north-west was:

Kelly's ale and Kelly's bread
Will keep you alive until you're dead.

When Chris invited me to lunch at his Cambridge home I soon realised he was the man for the job. Despite having a foot in plaster he jointly cooked a splendid lunch with his wife, Vivien. Then, during lunch, he still managed to hobble to the wine cupboard several times to furnish another bottle for us 'to try'. His puddings, calculated to turn health fanatics apoplectic, are his *pièce de résistance*. Grown men have been known to grow considerably further after consuming them – I speak from personal experience.

For this book Chris has visited a Scottish fish smokery, Smithfield Market, a game dealer, an organic farm and an English orchard. You will find he has emerged from this culinary assault course with flying colours. Chris also writes about the occasion when Prue Leith was challenged to run a British Rail buffet, an idea he came up with. Prue's recipes are also included and I think you'll find them well worth trying.

I very much hope you enjoy using this book as a practical part of your enjoyment of food and drink, whether for shopping, cooking or eating. The overture, you might well say, has gone on long enough. On with the first act . . .

Peter Bazalgette
Producer of *Food and Drink*

May 1987

SHERRY

THE SHERRY REVOLUTION
JILL GOOLDEN

Jill set out to discover the real sherry as the Spaniards drink it. What are the different types and where can you buy them? How should they be served?

'I thought it was all sticky and brown...' 'Only drunk at funerals...' 'An old people's drink'... When we took some delicious, genuine dry sherries to a London discotheque and offered them round, these were some of the comments *before* the revellers had a chance to try the chilled pale dry fino we produced like magicians straight from an insulated bag, and the rich, though still dry (a marvellous combination) oloroso we had brought along as well.

The impression of sherry after a few sips was a very different one in that discotheque that night, I can assure you. Nine out of ten drinkers who tried the new (to them) drinks were all for abandoning their cocktails with blue parasols and moving straight on to the dry sherries instead. I wasn't in the least surprised.

Dry sherry, which is the genuine article, is a deliciously satisfying drink, with the sort of taste that deserves to have a considerably wider appeal. The fact that it is little known and little drunk is not the customers' fault; it's because it is little mentioned, little seen and little sold.

But there is nothing unusual about *dry* sherry in the southwestern corner of Spain where all the best sherry is made. There sherry is enjoyed like wine, sipped as an aperitif, drunk with meals – and certainly enjoyed in discotheques, where refreshing fino sherry is served straight from the fridge in half bottles.

Since time immemorial though, sherry, 'the British drink', has been sweet; sweetened up specially for the supposedly sweet British taste, and, in the early days, to help it keep longer. Sugar, of course, acts as a preservative, highly necessary on sherry's long journey in the hold of a galleon on its way to the thirsty Brits. It is likely that sweet sherry has been coming to Britain for as long as 500 years.

And it has taken that long for the sherry shippers, a thoroughly conservative lot, to come round to the idea that we might actually prefer the refreshingly dry, subtle, *real* Spanish alternatives instead. At last, we are beginning to be offered a choice. Dry sherries in all shades, from the palest, transparent straw-coloured, through amber and conker to mahogany, are finally becoming widely available. I very strongly suggest, whatever your preconceptions about sherry might be, that you give them a try. Real sherry is a truly delicious drink.

The invention of wine is attributed to Noah in the Bible. (No, don't worry, I'm not going solemnly to chronicle the history of wine from the time of the Great Flood.) But sherry is *such* an ancient drink, I wouldn't be surprised to learn that he had a hand in the development of sherry too. Historians have traced the vine in the sherry-making region of Spain back to the sixth or fifth century BC, leaving an enormously long time for the Andalusians to perfect the art of making their fortified wine.

Spanish sherry is the prototype of all sherries, and unquestionably the best. In fact, anything labelled simply 'sherry' is certain to be the Real Macoy, because the Spaniards fought for the exclusive right to the name sherry. All imitators from elsewhere have to declare their origins as well, as in Cyprus sherry, for example. Now you know what to look for.

The corner of Spain inland from Cadiz has the perfect conditions for growing the right grapes, in the right inhospitable soil, and the right atmosphere mysteriously to encourage the development of certain 'freak' conditions which make real sherry unique. Man does not make sherry single-handed. Nature plays an extraordinary – and quite unpredictable – part as well.

To start with, the process for making sherry, with a few unusual twists, is much like that for making any other wine. Once the grapes are gathered in, they are first allowed to lie in the sun for a while (one of the 'twists'), before being pressed and taken to the *bodegas* (above-ground cellars) to be fermented in oak barrels. Come the new year, the young wine is separated from the sediment that has been thrown during fermentation.

But from then on the development of the wine varies quite dramatically from cask to cask, resulting in several completely different types of sherry, although it all started life the same. This is nature's contribution. Man has picked up a few tricks along the way, too, and he can now predetermine a certain amount himself. But he can't transport the sherry-making phenomenon successfully to other countries, which is why Spanish sherry is in a class on its own.

The 'phenomenon' is the spontaneous arrival on the surface of the wine of a curious blanket of a yeasty substance known as *flor*. Flor actually means flower, but not because of any similarity in appearance to its namesake. It in fact looks rather revolting, almost pure white and a mass of irregular wrinkles puckering up on top of the wine. But it works wonders, and transforms the wine underneath quite miraculously, without tainting it in the least. The flor elects to settle in certain barrels or casks in the spring, and with its welcome arrival, the wine is rather romantically said to 'flower'.

The effect of the blanket of flor is to feed on any remaining sugars left in the wine after fermentation, making it into potentially the driest wine in the world. (The act of fermentation itself is simply the consuming of sugar by yeasts, transforming it into alcohol.) At the same time the flor prevents oxygen from getting to the wine and oxidising it, which darkens the colour and alters the taste.

The wine attracting the growth of flor in the cask is destined to become either a **fino**, a pale, delicate, astringently dry sherry, clean, complex and refreshing, or a slightly fuller-bodied, darker, marginally heavier **amontillado**. Amontillados are usually sweetened for the British market to become 'medium' sherries.

Flor only elects to develop in some casks, leaving others virtually untouched. The wines in the casks without flor develop rather differently, and eventually become **olorosos**. (Oloroso means 'fragrant'.) Olorosos sold in this country are again habitually sweetened, to become sweet or cream sherries, but even these in their birthplace are naturally dry.

An oloroso starts life in Spain little darker than a fino, but as it matures, it gradually takes on more colour and depth, becoming an altogether heavier sherry. It is higher in alcohol as well. All sherries are fortified, meaning they have brandy added to make them more alcoholic than ordinary wines; olorosos are fortified more than finos.

So far I have described the heads of two family trees: fino and oloroso. Somewhere in the middle lies another sort of sherry, neither one thing nor another (but none the worse for its compromised position) **Palo cortado** is a compromise, like an oloroso, it grows little flor in cask, but it develops differently in other ways, becoming a light, fresh, dry sherry with a deep, intense bouquet.

Until recently palo cortados were hardly known over here, but we've got the message at last and they are becoming quite widely available. They've even been cited in the gossip columns as a classic 'yuppie' tipple. This means they've ARRIVED.

In the new wave of sherries, even a 'medium' is dry. In Jerez, its Spanish birthplace, ALL sherry starts off dry, and that includes amontillado. A true amontillado is an aged fino, and while whiling away its time in an oak cask for eight years or so, it becomes darker, fuller, softer and nuttier – intensely nutty if you taste one of the unsweetened examples. (The boast of the new '1796' range of Harvey's sherries is that they are all dry, and the range includes a proper dry amontillado.)

To transform all these subtle, complex, often pungent drinks into the sweet versions we are accustomed to, sweetening wines may be added, traditionally made from a grape grown especially to make sweet wines, the Pedro Ximenez. Because the sweetening wines add taste and colour to the wine as well as sweetness, they have to be chosen very carefully. Pale cream sherry, which claims to be a sweet fino (which is, of course, a contradiction in terms), has to be sweetened with a special kind of sugar to retain the attractive pale straw colour. But fino was never really meant to be sweetened, and in my opinion the end result is an unfortunate compromise.

So, as we've already seen, the process used to make sherry breaks rank with the traditional wine-making practice in the new year following the harvest, when the 'flor' arrives. The new wine is allowed to relax for a while in oak barrels or butts until inspected by the foreman of the *bodega*, whose job it is to predict the likely course the wine in each butt will take. Using a flexible whippy wand with a narrow silver cup at one end and a hook at the other called a *venencia*, he is able to draw out samples of the wine from deep inside each butt, scrutinise them for evidence of flor and its effects, and then make his prediction.

At this stage, all the wines will naturally be between 14 and 16% alcohol, which is pretty powerful for ordinary wines. This is because the sugar content of the grapes has been concentrated while they lay in the sun, and all of it has been converted into alcohol by the yeast. Generally when making table wines there is a lower level of sugar present in the grape juice, and this is not always fully fermented out. Looking at the contents of his *venencia* the foreman will discover that the wine in some barrels is developing flor and will be tending towards the lighter style, while in other butts little flor will be present, and the wine will be beginning to take on a heavier character.

The foreman then turns his prediction for each barrel into a self-fulfilling prophecy by adding a specific quantity of grape alcohol or brandy. Into the casks he judges are on their way to becoming finos, if necessary, he brings up the alcohol content to 15% or thereabouts, which is sufficiently high to kill off unwanted bugs and prevent them from spoiling the sherry. To the other casks, he adds a greater dollop of spirit, beefing the alcohol content up to 18%, which not only kills off the unwanted bugs, but any vestiges of flor as well. By the addition of alcohol he can affect nature's course, but he still cannot overrule the great force altogether because, although he can prevent flor from growing in some barrels, he is unable to promote it in others.

The local governing body in charge of sherry production in Jerez rules that sherry can be sold at anything between 15.5% and 17.5% alcohol. And in the local towns, where the Andalusians like to tipple away at their beloved finos any time of the day, the fino generally remains at the lower strength of 15.5% for the rest of its life. But, showing a tiresome streak of over-caution, the EEC decided to restrict the export of these '*bodega*-strength' finos, deciding they were not safe to travel unless fortified up to the top whack of 17%. It was our loss.

There is a delicious delicacy to lower-strength finos, which are very pale, light and streamlined; they have a gorgeous penetrating bouquet and a wonderfully refreshing, complex taste, which is unmasked by too much spirit. And the good news is that the 17.5% minimum rule has finally been waived and we are now officially allowed to receive these lower-strength finos over here. Slowly, but surely, they are beginning to filter on to the shelves. All will certainly proclaim their strength on the label (although this is not common practice with all sherries). So keep your eyes peeled and give them a try.

HOW TO MAKE THE MOST OF SHERRY

One of the reasons sherry's popularity has tended to slip is that it is usually served so *appallingly badly*. Most of the stuff you receive in your glass is actually off. The cause behind this dreadful state of affairs is ignorance; new ignorance coupled with old ignorance based on ill-founded traditions that have been allowed to persist.

The factors conspiring to ruin your enjoyment of a glass of sherry – especially when served in a pub – are:

1 It's often not fresh
2 It's usually at the wrong temperature
3 It's frequently served in an unsuitable glass.

So how can these simple wrongs be put right? I'll tell you – *with the greatest of ease.*

1 *Making sure it's fresh*: Sherry is essentially a wine. Admittedly there is a bit of brandy in it as well, but the major part is wine. And as we well know, wine, like milk, goes off. And, the lighter and drier the sherry, the quicker it will deteriorate. The effect of air on wine is eventually to turn it to vinegar. If you leave a bottle of ordinary table wine open for, say, 24 hours, next time you taste it you'll notice it is starting to taste sour, and after another day or two, it'll be virtually undrinkable. And it's not very different with sherry, except that sherry doesn't deteriorate quite as fast.

A bottle of sherry cannot be expected to keep indefinitely once opened. And, if you transfer the contents into a decanter, it's deterioration is actually speeded up. The solution is to finish the bottle before it starts to taste coarse and unpleasant. This is roughly how long each type of sherry will keep:

Fino: 10 days to 2 weeks, preferably kept in the fridge. The low-strength finos (15.5% and 16%), only 4 to 5 days.

Amontillado: 1 month to 6 weeks. Dry amontillado, 2 to 3 weeks.

Palo cortado: Maximum 2 weeks.

Oloroso: Sweet oloroso or cream sherries will stay in good order for about 3 months. The dry olorosos should be finished within 2 to 3 weeks.

2 *The right temperature*: Getting the temperature of a bottle of sherry or wine right doesn't mean harping back to some outdated rule of etiquette. Far from it. It means giving any bottle the chance to taste as good as possible, served as its maker intended. For all the lightest, most delicate finos (and in this instance I'll include pale creams in the same category) that means *chilled*.

Sadly this piece of advice is followed by so few people; even more lamentably, in so few pubs, restaurants and bars that it is perhaps complete news to you. But I assure you, it makes all the difference to the taste and enjoyment of the drink. To serve a fino sherry at room temperature is as much of a travesty – and does as much to ruin the taste – as pouring a warm glass of champagne.

For other sherries, room temperature – nothing fancy, just serving the bottle as is – is best.

3 *The right glass:* If ever you order a glass of sherry in a pub, you'll be given it in a schooner or waisted funnel ... perhaps the most unsuitable glass on earth. It is a ludicrous shape which seems purpose-designed to show off sherry at its absolute *worst*. One of the most enjoyable features of all sherries is the marvellous bouquet, and this is virtually lost in the schooner. Pour the same drink into a balloon or tulip-shaped glass, filled only to the halfway mark, and you'll be able to understand what I mean. The scent of the drink will well up and fill the space at the top of the glass, so that when you go to sip it, you can't help but get a full blast of the bouquet as well.

It would cost the big brewers and pub owners dear to scrap their dreadful schooners and kit themselves out with proper sherry *copitas*, as they are called. I appreciate that. But mere money shouldn't hold them back. Every time a glass of sherry is served in a schooner in a pub, nothing short of murder is being committed, and they should be mindful of that.

Where to find the new wave sherries

The key words to look for on the labels (front and back) of dry amontillados and olorosos are:
dry (*seco*),
very dry (*muy seco*),
very old (*muy viejo*).
Sometimes labels slip through with this vital information missing, in which case you will have to rely on the shop manager to guide you.

Palo cortados speak for themselves and are becoming widely available. The new, delicious, lower-strength finos can be spotted simply by looking on the label for an indication of percentage (meaning 'percentage of alcohol') *below* 17%.

Prices start at about £4, which is in fact very reasonable when you consider that many of these sherries are the very best that you can get, some containing wines perhaps as old as a century or more.

A taste of the new wave

The key sherries to look out for now are virtually all *dry*.

Fino: Palest hay colour, very delicate, piercingly fresh and astringently dry. The scent is fleetingly flowery, and there can be an almost salty quality – at its most noticeable in Manzanilla fino, which comes from the seaside Andalusian town of Sanlúcar de Barrameda.

Dry amontillado: From amber to auburn in colour. Powerful nutty scent, with a promise of a richness to come. And the richness is apparently there in the flavour, but the wine is quite dry, leaving it clean and uncloying; full-bodied and with great depth of flavour. A good dry sherry for self-confessed 'sweet tooths' to try.

Palo cortado: Almost a cross between the above two sherries, although a style in its own right. Richer than a fino and slighter than a dry amontillado.

Dry oloroso: Young oloroso is pale golden like fino, and it becomes darker and darker with time. Oloroso means 'fragrant', and this sherry lives up to its name with an intense pungency derived from the wine and the years spent in oak casks. Although dry, again the taste has a richness to it and there is even an apparently sweet aftertaste. This type of sherry is generally stronger in alcohol than the others.

SMOKED FISH

INTRODUCTION
CHRIS KELLY

Chris went up to Scotland to discover the truth about smoked salmon and other smoked fish. Here are the results of his research.

As late as the turn of the century, Scottish servants would have it written into their contracts that they wouldn't be forced to eat salmon more than twice a week. Imagine the scene, as they trooped into the bowels of the house, dog-weary after a day of blacking grates and beating carpets. There, in the middle of the table, lies a magnificent specimen of *Salmo salar*, a 12-pounder, poached to perfection and garnished with cucumber and love by Mrs McCheeryoldsoul. And what do the servants cry? Do we hear the echo of hallelujahs the length of Union Street? Do the sedate granite mansions ring to their joyous acclaim? Not a bit ot it: 'Oh no, not salmon again!' is the ingrates' universal howl, and poor Mrs McCheeryoldsoul is obliged to devour the entire dish herself.

When salmon prices are often beyond our budget, it's difficult to grasp the fact that 'the King of fish', as the brochures are fond of calling it, was once extraordinarily plentiful. In 1776, on the Tweed, over 700 salmon were taken in a single haul of the net; and more than a century earlier, on a June night in 1648, one pool on the Findhorn yielded almost twice that number. Nor were the Scots selfish about sharing their abundant delicacy; as far back as the fourteenth century they were exporting it to faraway Livorno and Venice, fresh-packed in straw baskets, or pickled and salted in wooden containers.

Despite the much-diminished availability of salmon – and partly, perhaps, because of it – the fish has an enduring appeal: its epic journeys to and from the spawning grounds remain mysterious; it is beautiful, versatile and simple to cook; its delicate flavour and texture are unique; it is a star. For these reasons, among others, the salmon was the focus of my visit to the Aberdeen headquarters of fish merchants Allan and Dey, leaders in the export field. They would tell me – if anyone could – why Scottish smoked fish, and specifically salmon, is generally regarded as the best in the world. (The drive in from the airport was enough to whet the appetite: fly-fishermen were up to their knees in the broad river Dee, whose grassy banks were flooded with daffodils.)

The two Allan and Dey factories were founded in 1890 by local worthies Councillor Dey and Baillie Allan, who sound as sturdy as the grey stone of the city. The factories lie beside the fish market, operating seven days a week and employing 250.

While the twentieth century has brought sophisticated advances in chilling, packaging and marketing techniques, the basic business of preparing fish for the smoking process has changed little. On the ground floor at Allan and Dey, standing on duckboards to keep their feet out of the worst of the wet, lines of aproned cutters with sharp knives behead, slice and gut haddock caught only the day before off Lerwick. (On the executive floor, there are sepia blow-ups of the cutters' Victorian predecessors doing exactly the same job in much the same way.) The central trough in front of them is brimming with cold, bloody water, and beside each worker is a bucket of hot water into which the knife is regularly plunged.

Beyond the lines, there is at last evidence that the scene belongs to a period after – rather than before – the Industrial Revolution: fish-splitting and filleting machines share the space with the human workers. The machines, all German-made, with the exception of a single, irreplaceable British model, create such a racket that the cutters have to shout to be heard.

After undergoing its initial surgery, the haddock is brined and coloured (if that's the way the customer prefers it) in a great tub containing the natural dye annatto. The mixture looks like a vat of mulligatawny soup. (Increasingly consumers, wary of some E numbers, are calling for undyed fish.) Four minutes later, the haddock emerges, dripping, and is then drained on trays before going into the kiln. Soon these same fillets will be on sale in shops and markets as far afield as the United States and Canada. By the time they appear on plates in Boston or Toronto, they will have been blast frozen and de-frosted, but it's no surprise to learn that the French insist on buying their smoked fish fresh.

Haddock is only a small part of Allan and Dey's large range. They also deal in kippers, coley (much favoured in the Irish Republic), ling, cod, scallops, tusk, finnan haddock, mackerel and highly prized monkfish. (The day I was there, monkfish was fetching £100 per 8-stone box in the early morning wholesale market. When you consider that the removal of the massive head leaves only 40% of the original fish, the fact that it sells to the consumer at a premium is understandable.)

The industrious production line proves to be only a curtain-raiser for the main event. At the back of the filleting hall, in a small bare room, four blue-overalled figures in white hats are working on the most glamorous fish in the factory. Ice and running water, much of it scarlet with salmon blood, are everywhere. This is a process which cannot be hurried. At every stage, impressive care is taken to make sure the product emerges as perfect looking and tasting smoked salmon.

First, the head of the great silver fish is unceremoniously removed and two patches of skin are shaved off each of the flanks, so when salt is applied it penetrates the flesh. Next, with a knife like a small machete, the salmon is split down the middle and gutted, leaving the backbone attached to one side; this is then skilfully sliced away so that not a shred of valuable meat is wasted. With a finer blade, the secondary bones are cut out, and any remaining blood is squeezed from tiny veins by hand to prevent discoloration in the kiln. Now the salmon is ready for sprinkling with large-grain salt, which gently melts into the sides over the next 12 to 15 hours.

The following morning, the salmon is immersed in water and scrubbed clean of salt before being laid on racks in an adjoining room, where it will dry for up to 4 hours. Nearly 500 sides a day are processed like this, beginning a journey which could end in any one of countless cities around the world hungry for Scottish smoked salmon.

The art of smoking fish has been perfected in Scotland over hundreds of years. The 'Torry' kilns used by Allan and Dey were developed by a local research station, but their basic principle is as old as the industry. They stand upstairs at the factory in a solid phalanx, like bank vaults. Beside them is a rather insignificant-looking little stove with an electric plate at its base and a blackened chimney, joining it to the kilns where the fish sides hang expectantly. As the heat from the plate warms the pine sawdust (or, in the case of salmon, oak chips) lying on it, dense smoke rises and, via the chimney, circulates round the neighbouring fish. This is known as *cold smoking*, where the fish is simply dried and given added flavour but remains uncooked. Salmon, for instance, is cold smoked. If the product is to be *hot smoked* it first undergoes the cold smoking process, then the temperature of the kiln is raised to 90°F (32°C) and for a further period, lasting perhaps an hour and a half, the fish actually cooks as it softly absorbs the smoke.

Released from its vault, the cold smoked salmon can be packaged or presented in a variety of ways. I watched Maureen Barry preparing a side for easy eating. Starting at the tail, she cut it deftly into 24 slices, leaving not a trace of flesh on the skin. She then reformed the fish, replacing it on its silver back, interleaving the slices with opaque paper. Slipped into a tartan plastic envelope, with a window, and a label pronouncing it 'quality approved' by the Scottish Salmon Smokers' Association, the fish was finally entombed in a vacuum-packer which, with a sharp 'whoosh', suddenly and magically made the opaque layers of paper disappear altogether.

So, after all that, what makes Scottish salmon taste better than the rest? I put the question to Sandy Ross, Allan and Dey's Factory Manager. Despite the fact that he spends up to £50,000 every week buying fresh fish, he still modestly describes himself as an 'ordinary sort of guy who gets up early and goes to bed late'. It turns out that he has no answer. It's the same with Scotch whisky, he says – something in the water, something in the centuries they've been producing it . . . something you can't describe. But then, he's not a man for hyperbole. Confront him with the awesome thought that on a good day he must oversee some 300 cwt of fish going through the factory and he simply says: 'Well, it keeps me occupied, shall I say.'

Those who would have you believe that they are purists, might be heard to claim that farmed salmon is in some way inferior to the wild variety. It's true wild salmon was fetching £1 per pound (450g) more at auction than farmed when I was in Aberdeen, but for all that, John Masson, Allan and Dey's managing director, prefers the latter. If you need to know the difference when the fish is fresh on the slab, farmed salmon is less torpedo-shaped than wild and is more heavily speckled along its back; in case of doubt, don't hesitate to ask your fishmonger.

John Masson estimates that by at least 1990 salmon farming will be generating as much at auction as the whole of the Scottish white fish industry put together. As a result, prices should come down, and 'the King of fish' will be offered in a greater variety of forms. With salmon in abundance once more the Scots may yet again be heard to complain, 'Oh no, not salmon again!'

Meanwhile, the best time to buy fresh salmon is from the beginning of June until the second week in August; the cheapest cut is the tail, which some say is the sweetest part of the fish. Smoked salmon will probably be less expensive at Easter than at other times, because producers may be happy to reduce stock to which they over-committed themselves at Christmas. They may also be eager to revive sales after the slow months of January and February.

> If you feel like side-stepping the middleman and buying salmon direct from the factory (where you should get it on better terms) you can write to, or telephone:
> Allan and Dey Limited,
> Raik Road,
> Aberdeen,
> Scotland AB9 2AG.
>
> Telephone: 0224 581000

RECIPES
MICHAEL BARRY

SMOKED SALMON SCRAMBLE
Serves 4

The king of smoked fishes, smoked salmon, really doesn't need much to help it along. But sometimes less expensive offcuts can be bought. Use them in my special favourite, smoked salmon scramble. This is a very luxurious way of serving scrambled eggs and is smashing for high tea, and also pretty good for dinner party starters in individual ramekins, to be eaten with buttered, crustless brown toast. You can make this with ordinary smoked salmon and not just offcuts, if you choose.

8 eggs
4 oz (100 g) smoked salmon pieces
3 oz (75 g) butter
Salt and freshly ground black pepper
Juice of 1 lemon
Fresh parsley sprigs, to garnish

Beat the eggs together in a bowl, then finely chop 1 oz (25 g) smoked salmon and mix in. You can mix them together in a food processor to save trouble, if you like. Melt the butter in a thick, preferably non-stick frying pan. (Please don't cut down on the quantity, or use a substitute; the texture and flavour can be destroyed if you do.) Before it stops sizzling, pour in the egg and salmon mixture and stir gently to make soft scrambled eggs.

As soon as the whole of the mixture is thick and curdled, season generously, being careful, however, with the salt if the salmon's very salty, and squeeze in the lemon juice. Stir again and spoon into individual ramekins or on top of rounds of wholemeal toast. Decorate with the remaining smoked salmon, cut into matchstick slivers and sprinkled over the tops. A little parsley on top adds a touch of colour, but you don't need much lest it alter the flavour.

SMOKED SALMON AND CAVIAR PANCAKES
Makes 8

This recipe's a bit of a cheat because it isn't *real* caviar I'm suggesting you use, but the very pretty red lumpfish roe, available in all the large supermarkets. It doesn't quite have caviar's flavour, but then it doesn't quite have caviar's price either, which seems to me to be an unanswerable advantage! You can make your own pancakes for this using the batter I suggest on page 46, making about ten 6-inch (15-cm) round, thick pancakes, or you can use ready-made pancakes.

In Russia, where the original of this crafty dish came from, they used yeast pancakes and black caviar, but they left out the smoked salmon. I think you will find this was a mistake.

**8 pancakes, approximately 6 inches (15 cm) round,
and thick if possible
1 small jar red lumpfish roe
1 5 oz (150 g) carton sour cream
4 oz (100 g) smoked salmon pieces**

If your pancakes aren't freshly made, wrap them very loosely in foil and heat them in a medium oven, about 350°F (180°C), gas mark 4, for 10 minutes, until hot.

Meanwhile, stir the lumpfish roe into the sour cream, and cut the smoked salmon pieces into thin slivers. (You can use proper smoked salmon slices for this, it's just more expensive.)

When the pancakes are hot, put them on warm plates and spread a layer of the sour cream mixture over each, then sprinkle the centres with some of the smoked salmon. The sour cream should come to within ½ inch (1 cm) of the edge of each pancake and the smoked salmon should form a little heap in the middle. Serve immediately.

SMOKED MACKEREL PÂTÉ
Serves 4–6

Smoked mackerel has become the most popular of the smoked fish eaten in England. There was a time when kippers had this honour, but with the overfishing of the herring population, people began to discover how well – as an alternative – mackerel took to the same process. In fact there are two kinds of smoked mackerel: *hot* and *cold* smoked. The hot smoked is the one that's normally used for pâtés. It is possible to eat the cold smoked variety, the one that's treated in the same way as kippers and smoked salmon, raw – just as kippers and smoked salmon can be eaten raw – but it doesn't make a very good pâté.

This recipe uses hot smoked mackerel and is very simple to make, particularly if you have a blender or food processor. You can also make it by hand with very little extra effort. Just make sure that you soak the slices of white bread long enough for them to break up and crumble easily.

You can serve this as a starter and it's also great for a picnic, still in its pot so that it can be scooped out with a spoon and dolloped on to crusty French bread.

1 thick slice white bread, crust removed
Approximately 4 tablespoons milk
2 large fillets hot smoked mackerel, skinned
Juice of ½ lemon
2 oz (50 g) butter, melted
1 tablespoon chopped fresh dill,
or 1 heaped teaspoon dried dill or parsley
2 tablespoons natural yoghurt, or fromage frais

Soak the bread in the milk until it's saturated. Put the mackerel into a blender or food processor and mix until it's a smooth paste, then add all the other ingredients and mix for 10 seconds. Scrape the mixture down and mix for a further 5 seconds. Serve the pâté piled high in individual ramekins, or in a soufflé dish with the surface smoothed over. Serve with wholemeal toast or hot French bread.

NOTE: If you want to keep the pâté for more than 2 days, cover with a thin layer of melted butter and store in the fridge covered tightly with foil; it will last up to 1 week.

KIPPERS

Whenever kippers are spoken of there is invariably a great dispute about whether to eat them raw or not and, if you cook them, how to do it. I'm very fond of the taste of raw kippers, but I've only ever once had them raised to real gourmet level and that was at a buffet put on by Michelin to launch one of their British guidebooks. The *Michelin Guide* has a tremendous culinary reputation and the kippers were certainly up to it. They had been filleted *very* carefully, sliced across the grain and mixed with very thinly sliced blanched onions, then dressed in good fruity olive oil and lots of black pepper and marinated for at least 6 hours. Done that way, they became a luxury item, which I suspect they would always have been if we hadn't got used to having them so plentifully in the first half of the century.

As far as cooking them is concerned, there are two quite separate schools – one says grill and the other says poach. I'm for the grilling method, which involves pre-heating the grill until it is very hot and lining the grill pan with foil so there's no nasty washing up afterwards. Spread the kippers with butter rather like toast, cut side up, before popping them under the grill until they're crispy brown on the edges. Then the key is to eat them immediately, pouring over the juices caught in the foil.

The poaching method is rather like making tea and involves filling a heatproof jug large enough to hold the kippers upright, full of boiling water. Dunk the kippers, head first, in and leave them for 5 minutes, then take them up, put them on a warm plate, spread a little butter over them to melt and serve immediately. I find this method removes some of the intense smoky flavour, and if you like your food mild you might just prefer it.

CULLEN SKINK
Serves 4
A quite extraordinary name for a very delicious fish soup that's never made it south of the border until recently. I don't know why,

as it uses one of the most popular smoked fish and is very easy to make indeed. I've suggested using a finnan haddock, which is the one with the bones in, but any golden smoked fish makes an extremely pleasant soup in this particular style. It's very warming and ideal for a cold blustery day.

You can, by the way, make this soup with half the fish meat off an ordinary finnan haddock and eat the rest at the time you cook it, or mash it up and use as a base for poached eggs on granary toast – a delicious combination – or even as a filling for an omelette. An omelette with cooked finnan haddock as a filling, sprinkled with Parmesan cheese, was made famous by the literary giant Arnold Bennett.

1 smoked finnan haddock,
or 1 lb (450 g) ordinary haddock, skinned
1 pint (600 ml) milk
1 lb (450 g) potatoes, peeled and cut in ½-inch (1-cm) cubes
8 oz (225 g) onions, chopped
Salt and freshly ground pepper
Chopped fresh parsley

Poach the haddock in the milk for 20 minutes, then remove the skin and bones, and flake. Poach the potatoes and onions in the same milk for 15 minutes, until the potatoes are tender. Season (gently with the salt). Add the flaked haddock to the milk, then serve hot with parsley sprinkled over the top. It should be a soup, so if it is too thick, thin down with water or more milk and re-heat.

KEDGEREE
Serves 4–6

There is much argument about this dish. It's certain that it emerged from India in the nineteenth century and was a common thing on the tiffin tables of the rulers of the raj, but its exact nature is much disputed. There is an Indian dish called khichri, also made with rice, but with lentils instead of smoked haddock.

Even the kedgeree we eat in Britain has a number of versions. This is the one I've found easiest and it makes not only a delicious breakfast dish for the truly hungry, but also a marvellous weekend brunch centrepiece, as you can easily make it in quite large quantities.

8 oz (225 g) smoked haddock and/or cod
½ pint (300 ml) milk
8 oz (225 g) long-grain rice
1 small onion, chopped
1 teaspoon mild (or home-made) curry powder
2 oz (50 g) butter
4 hard-boiled eggs, quartered, to garnish
1½-inch (4-cm) piece cucumber, very thinly sliced, to garnish
Mango chutney, to serve (optional)

Poach the fish in the milk for about 10 minutes or until it flakes easily. Drain, reserving the milk, then flake the fish, discarding any skin and bones. Measure the rice in a cup, then put it in a saucepan and add the milk the fish was cooked in and enough water to make double the quantity of liquid to rice. Cook over a moderate heat until all the liquid is absorbed and the rice is tender.

In a separate pan, very gently fry the onion with the curry powder in the butter for 5 minutes. Add the rice, the flaked fish and gently stir until thoroughly mixed together, taking care not to break up the fish too much. Turn into a serving dish and garnish with the hard-boiled eggs and cucumber. Maybe not entirely authentic, but it's great served with mango chutney.

For those of you who really can't stomach the distinctive flavour of smoked fish (I hope only a few) here are a couple of recipes using non-smoked fish.

MRS BEETON'S RECIPE
FOR COD IN EGG SAUCE
TRANSLATED INTO CRAFTY COOKING

It was the 150th anniversary of Mrs Beeton's birth in 1986 and to celebrate we looked up some recipes in the facsimile edition of her cookery book. Most 'Mrs Beeton' books these days don't have many recipes that actually passed through her hands. But the facsimile edition is fascinating because it demonstrates a life-style and a range of food we very rarely associate with the Victorians. They ate not only heartily, but a surprising number of different cuisines. There are Malaysian, Indian, South American and South African dishes, all cheek by jowl with standard English fare in the original Mrs Beeton. She collected her recipes from all over the world from many correspondents and didn't pretend to have tested them all herself. This particular one, however, I think she probably did try because her comments on how to cook fresh cod seem to me to come from personal experience.

In one respect I take issue with Mrs Beeton, who suggested the eggs in the sauce should be coarsely chopped. I tried that and didn't like it. I suggest you finely chop the hard-boiled eggs and if you don't fancy the hard-boiled egg sauce, which is in fact delicious but very rich, you could try a slightly different version of parsley sauce with a few thinly sliced leeks in it (see below).

1 cod fillet per person
1 teaspoon salt per fish fillet
1 lemon slice per fish fillet
Finely chopped fresh parsley, to garnish

Egg sauce
4 oz (100 g) butter
1 dessertspoon cornflour
Scant 7 fl oz (200 ml) cold water
Juice of ½ lemon
4 hard-boiled eggs, finely chopped

Rub each piece of fish with salt and set aside for 30 minutes. Mrs Beeton believed this firmed the fish and stopped it being watery. Wash off the salt and carefully skin the fish with a sharp knife. Place each slice of fish on a lemon slice in a gratin dish and cover with buttered foil. Bake at 350°F (180°C), gas mark 4, for 20 minutes, until the fish is cooked through.

Meanwhile, make the sauce. Place the butter, cornflour and water in the top of a double boiler over boiling water, and stir in one direction only until thick. Add the lemon juice and eggs. Let the sauce heat through. Serve hot on top of the baked fish, garnished with a sprinkling of parsley.

Leek and Parsley Sauce
½ pint (300 ml) White Sauce made from
½ pint (300 ml) milk, 1 oz (25 g) plain flour and 1 oz (25 g) butter
8 oz (225 g) leeks, very thinly sliced and washed
1 handful fresh parsley sprigs, finely chopped
Salt and freshly ground black pepper
Squeeze of lemon juice (optional)

Stir the milk, flour and butter together while cold in a non-stick saucepan. Heat gently, whisking every 30 seconds or so, until the sauce is smooth and thick. Add the leeks and simmer for 5 minutes, then add the parsley and season to taste. A squeeze of lemon juice can sometimes liven the sauce up a little bit, but it's very bright green and rich as it comes. (Incidentally, without the leeks, this is *the* crafty way of making béchamel sauce.)

SKATE IN BLACK BUTTER
Serves 2

Many of the fish we have little regard for are highly prized in other parts of the world, particularly just across the Channel in France. One of these is ray, or skate as we call it. It tends to be one of the cheaper fish in our fish and chip shops and is hardly seen on menus otherwise. But it makes one of the classic dishes of northern France when served with what they call a 'black butter' sauce.

One of the advantages of skate is that it doesn't have conventional bones. Instead, the wings have long, thin tendons running through them. You can ignore and discard these but the French regard them as a delicacy, as they're very easy to crunch and don't have any nasty, splintery effects. They add what is described as 'extra texture' to the fish. The black butter sauce is not meant to be black at all, so be warned. At most, it's meant to be a pale hazelnut colour, and the slight 'catching' of the butter gives it an appropriately nutty flavour.

Serve very quickly straight out of the pan, on to hot plates. It's not a dish that likes to be kept waiting and doesn't go very well with chips either. It's much better to serve a separate vegetable dish afterwards or, at most, boiled new potatoes with it. French bread to mop up the juices is, however, an excellent idea.

1 lb (450 g) wing of skate
1 pint (600 ml) water
1 small onion, stuck with cloves
4 black peppercorns
1 bay leaf
1 lemon slice
Pinch of salt
4 oz (100 g) unsalted butter
2 tablespoons cider or wine vinegar
2 teaspoons capers, well drained

Put the skate in a large frying pan into which it will fit flat. Pour over the water and add the onion, peppercorns, bay leaf, lemon slice and salt. Bring to the boil, turn down to a very low simmer, cover and cook for about 15 minutes, until the flesh on the top flakes easily. Drain carefully and place the fish on a hot plate and cover to keep it warm.

Discard the poaching liquid and flavourings. Melt the butter in the same pan and let it heat until it just starts to turn brown and gives off a slightly nutty aroma. *Don't let it burn.* Pour the butter over the fish and add the vinegar and capers to the unwashed pan. Boil for about 10 seconds and then pour over the fish and serve immediately. The combination of the juicy fish, the slightly nutty butter and the sharpness of the vinegar and the capers is what gives this dish its legendary reputation.

D R I N K S
JILL GOOLDEN

SIMPLE GUIDE TO BUYING WHITE WINE
White wines and rosés are the classic wines to accompany fish. Jill tells you what to look out for.

Choosing white and rosé wines in some supermarkets and high street wine shops has now been considerably simplified by the introduction of the White Wine Taste Guide, which simply numbers wines in order of their dryness/sweetness. The most instantly apparent difference between one white wine and another is its relative sweetness and the judgement of this is one of the taste buds' four basic skills. (The other three are to assess sourness, bitterness and saltiness.)

It's quite simple to assess if a wine is dry, medium or sweet once you have tasted it; less easy, in most cases, if you have only the outside of the bottle to go by. This guide, however, devised by an independent body – the Wine Development Board – solves that problem by numbering wines on a scale of 1 to 9 according to their apparent sweetness. The guide appears either on the wine's label or on the shop shelf.

Number **1** signifies the driest wine you can get; **2** slightly less astringently dry; **3** edging out of the bone-dry camp; **4** beginning to soften into a medium; **5** definitely medium; **6** getting a bit sweeter, and so on until you reach the sweetest wines, which carry the number **9**.

If you know more or less what you are looking for on the dryness/sweetness scale, you can therefore easily be guided to a wine you will like – and one to suit the meal you are preparing. There are other qualities that contribute to the total taste of a white or rosé wine as well, such as weight or body and concentration of flavour, but these are learned by experience.

The White Wine Taste Guide has been adopted by a great number of shops selling wine but regrettably it is not used everywhere, although I can't see why on earth not. New wine consumers need all the help they can get, not just when buying wine to serve at home, but when choosing wine off a restaurant wine list as well.

How some well-known white and rosé wines fit into the scale:

1 Bergerac, Chablis, Champagne, Entre-deux-mers, Muscadet, Sancerre, Saumur, Tavel rosé, Touraine.

2 Chardonnays, dry Vouvray, Frascati, Graves, sparkling wines (Méthode Champenoise, Cava and Sekt), Orvieto Secco, Riesling d'Alsace, Soave, Trocken German wines, Verdicchio, white Burgundy, white Rioja.

3 Anjou rosé, brut sparkling wines, Gewürztraminer d'Alsace, Halbtrocken German wines, Muscat d'Alsace, medium-dry English wines, Pinot Blanc d'Alsace.

4 Australian, New Zealand and Bulgarian Rieslings, Chenin Blancs, EEC wines, German wines (of the Tafelwein, QbA and Kabinett quality), medium-dry Yugoslav Laski and Hungarian Olasz Riesling, Orvieto Abboccato, Vinho Verde, Portuguese rosés.

5 German wines of Spätlese quality, Liebfraumilch, Vouvray demi-sec.

6 Demi-sec Champagne and sparkling wines, medium Spanish wines.

7 Asti Spumante, German wines of Auslese quality, Monbazillac, Première Côtes-de-Bordeaux.

8 Barsac, German wines of Beerenauslese quality, Moscato wines, Sauternes, Spanish sweet wines.

9 German wines of Trockenbeerenauslese quality, Muscat de Beaumes de Venise and other sweet Muscats.

VEGETABLES

INTRODUCTION
CHRIS KELLY

ORGANIC VEGETABLES

Organic farming is booming as consumers want more pesticide-free produce. Yet one organic vegetable may not be the same as the next. Chris gives us the dirt on the organic movement.

Unquestionably, the big news on the vegetable front is the rapid growth in demand and production of organic vegetables. We have to import 60% of the organically grown produce we consume, but the organic movement is rapidly gaining new British members. It has been estimated that by the year 2000, about 7% of British food production will be organic. Currently it's closer to 0.5%.

Well great, I hear you cry, but just what does 'organic' mean? The word shines like a beacon in a naughty world and yet most of us, I fancy, would have great difficulty in defining it. We probably first became vaguely aware of the concept in the sixties and seventies; then, in the popular imagination, it summoned up visions of pale people in sandals living in things called communes.

Chambers 20th Century Dictionary defines organic as 'produced without, or not involving, the use of fertilisers and pesticides not wholly of plant or animal origin'. That is helpful, but in order to understand the word in a wider context, we need to go back to 1946. In the spring of that year a number of individuals, concerned that soil might suffer long-term damage from chemicals used to promote intensive food production, launched the Soil Association, a charitable foundation with three main aims:

1 To bring together all those working for a fuller understanding of the vital relationships between soil, plant, animal and man.

2 To initiate, co-ordinate and help with research in this field.

3 To collect and distribute the knowledge gained, creating a body of informed public opinion.

The Soil Association had great early success. By the following year, membership had spread from Britain to the Commonwealth, the USA, Holland and France. In Denmark, the Bio-Dynamic Association, founded on broadly similar lines and based on the philosophy of Rudolf Steiner, was also winning support. There were, however, rocky times ahead. The association weathered the inflationary seventies largely thanks to its inspirational president, Dr E. F. Schumacher. He saw the need to demonstrate that organic farming wasn't just a pious hope, that organic farmers could actually earn a living by selling 'poison-free' food.

By the end of the decade there was an increasing public preoccupation with health. Aware of the dangers of heart disease and obesity, we began to ask a number of direct questions about the food we were eating. In particular, additives, such as colourings, preservatives and flavourings, came under scrutiny; in many cases manufacturers were forced to abandon them. More fundamentally, though, we started to voice misgivings about the ways foodstuffs were grown; about 'unseen additives', such as artificial fertilisers and chemical sprays. *The Times* on 30 October 1986 carried a piece about the findings of the Social and Community Planning Unit:

> A high level of concern about the fate of the countryside is shown among people questioned for the report. About a third professed themselves very concerned. The data suggests that all parties would benefit from the adoption of policies to protect the countryside. Pollution, whether industrial or agricultural, is seen as the greatest threat, with two thirds of the sample agreeing that modern farming methods damage the countryside.

Searching for an environmentally acceptable alternative means of production, more farmers and growers turned to the Soil Association for guidance. The association awards the use of its coveted symbol to those who comply with its strict standards, including an insistence that no soluble artificial fertiliser or agrochemical should have been used on the land during the previous two years. Inspectors carry out rigorous checks so you can be confident that vegetables or any other foodstuff bearing the Soil Association symbol have been grown as nature intended. There are currently just under 1000 symbol-holders, and the ranks are multiplying every year.

It's not unfair, therefore, to say that the Soil Association's recommended system is, in itself, a workable definition of organic. There are, however, other organisations with largely sympathetic but different standards. Organic Farmers and Growers, for instance, based in East Anglia, certify two standards considered to be organic: OFG 1, which is claimed to be 'totally organic', and the Conservation Grade for farmers who want to use fewer chemicals but are unwilling to settle for none. The latter has been severely criticised by the Soil Association but is now administered separately from the OFG organisation. Conservation Grade farmers are now restricted to materials tested by Wye Agricultural College as not leaving artificial residues in the soil or the food. But remember it is not a full 'organic' system. Farm Verified Organics, owned by an American company, also have their own scheme which is similar to that of the Soil Association but is restricted to FVO's subsidiaries and has no inspectorate. It could be held to be a form of branding; some people are worried about the potential for abuse where commercial concerns are responsible for policing themselves. To confuse matters still further, there is the International Demeter Scheme, run on the Bio-Dynamic principle, under which nearly 50% of all German and Dutch organic foodstuffs are produced. This is universally held to guarantee high standards and integrity, though few British farmers belong, and most who do are also members of the Soil Association. The International Federation of Organic Agriculture Movements is seeking to make a thorough assessment of the various schemes with a view to publishing a directory of the ones it approves.

So pity the poor consumer. What can be done to sort out the plethora of standards? Our own Ministry of Agriculture has now announced that 'Food from Britain' is to set up a single organic standard. All existing organisations will be checked to ensure that their rules meet minimum requirements, there will be inspectors and a single logo for the produce. There will also be a register of individual producers allowed to use the new logo.

It all sounds too good to be true, doesn't it? And predictably, there is a catch. The scheme is to be entirely voluntary. So any farmer who feels like it (and who plunges chemicals into his land) could conceivably misuse the label 'organic'. Let us hope that does not happen and that 'Food from Britain' are swift in their deliberations.

In the meantime, amidst all the organic confusion here are five symbols you can look out for

 The Soil Association

 The Demeter Scheme

 The Organic Farmers and Growers

 The Conservation Grade

 Farm Verified Organic

When organic vegetables were perceived as a fringe food, they were sold chiefly at the farm gate or in health food shops. Now they have found a niche in greengrocers' and supermarkets all over the country, though some buyers are slow, in the words of a Dublin University scientist, to 'tolerate the odd hole in carrots or some scab on apples'. It is a fact that if we want a regular, and readily available, supply of organically grown vegetables, we must relax our expectations of a cosmetically perfect product.

The introduction of organic produce to supermarkets was pioneered by Safeway, which claims in its Report to Employees to 'lead the industry with a range of organically grown produce, an added bonus for those customers who are looking for more healthy type products'.

Safeway's principal organic grower and supplier is Donald Cooper, a refugee from Surrey suburbia, who did well enough in the printing and packaging industry to take up organic farming as a hobby. In 1972, moving with his wife, Marie, to a Victorian farmhouse set in 30 acres of Kent, Donald left aside 5 acres for private gardens and grew cereals on the rest. Meanwhile, the London restaurants he frequented complained they were unable to find enough quality vegetables of the more unusual variety, especially mange tout. So Donald began to supply them. But word spread, and he was soon able to count Buckingham Palace among his customers. The corn fields shrank, the market garden expanded and Donald sought further outlets for his produce, which included haricots verts, red shallots, globe artichokes, fennel and Chinese leaves, still a novelty. Around 1980, Marie suggested they approach a supermarket. Donald telephoned the produce buyer at Safeway, who showed interest and a deal was done. The initial order was for six boxes of mange tout, delivered in a car boot. Now, drawing on the resources of a growers' co-operative, Donald supplies Safeway with 38 varieties of organically grown vegetables. He has 185 acres of organically grown produce and is the biggest organic farmer in Britain.

By the time Donald Cooper was awarded his Soil Association symbol, he had not used chemicals on his land for almost 10 years. 'If you are lucky enough to own or manage land,' he says, 'you have a moral responsibility to pass on that land to future generations in a good, healthy condition, and not poisoned with toxic chemicals.' Nevertheless, Donald was fortunate that he didn't start his farm in East Anglia, where, it has been estimated, some agricultural land is so impregnated with chemicals that purification might take 50 years. He claims organically grown produce not only has twice the shelf-life of the conventionally grown equivalents, but also has much more flavour. The reason, Donald says, is that the nitrogen content of the fertiliser used to speed the progress of conventionally raised vegetables actually promotes wet, sappy growth with little taste, whereas organically grown plants develop a heavier bulk at their own natural pace. Donald finds that weeds are the most difficult problem for the grower who rejects the use of agrochemicals. 'People with hoes cost more than sprays,' he says. However, the average premium of up to 30% which consumers are prepared to pay for organic produce should go some way towards compensating farmers.

Donald and committed growers like him emphasise that they're providing the consumer with choice, and the diet we choose is one of the few ways we can directly affect our own health and the quality – perhaps even the length – of our lives. These crucial considerations demand that the government and the EEC do more to encourage organic growing, yet at present there is only one small organic training course in Britain, at the Worcester College of Agriculture. Now that we can offer an alternative system to food grown with the use of chemicals, we have the power to change agricultural policies. Vegetables grown organically are more expensive than the conventional variety, but production in greater bulk should bring the price down. As Patrick Holden of the Soil Association points out, there is a 'hidden social cost' in modern conventional agriculture which many find much more unacceptable than a 30% premium. He includes in that phrase the colossal expense of EEC agrochemical policies, environmental damage and health threats. Since the present system fails us at so many levels, Patrick argues, why not support a natural, healthy means of production that works?

You'll find the most comprehensive list of retail outlets for organically grown food in *The New Organic Food Guide*. The Soil Association will send you a copy – write, enclosing a cheque or postal order for £4.45 (inc. p&p) made payable to The Soil Association, to:
The Soil Association,
86 Colston Street,
Bristol,
Avon BS1 5BB.

R E C I P E S
MICHAEL BARRY

Michael's recipes include two vegetarian dishes to satisfy any appetite, as well as plenty of ways for improving the flavour and texture of vegetables.

VEGETARIAN CASSOULET
Serves 4
Cassoulet is one of the great dishes of French cooking. As with so many of these dishes, it began as a rustic peasant meal in the

Languedoc – the south of France near Carcassonne. It is traditionally a meal-in-a-pot, a mixture of haricot beans (dried white beans),
various meats, tomatoes and flavourings baked for several hours to
produce a very rich, thick, savoury stew. This version, while main-
taining the slow baking and the rich savouriness, does not use any
meat. I replace it with a variety of vegetables and nuts to produce
the textures and nutrition the meat normally contributes. I and all
my family and friends actually prefer this vegetarian version. Either
way, with or without meat, a cassoulet is a really filling dish. Serve it
in soup plates or bowls, with a little French bread, and nothing
much to follow except a salad, perhaps a little cheese and some
fruit. For extra spiciness you could add some Tabasco sauce, so
long as you like hot food.

Be sure to allow yourself enough time to soak the haricot beans
and chestnuts; use a large bowl for the beans as they swell to almost
double in size.

1 lb (450 g) dried haricot beans, soaked for 6 hours
5 fl oz (150 ml) olive oil
4 tablespoons thick tomato purée
1 medium onion, studded with cloves
1 clove garlic, crushed
Large pinch each of dried oregano and thyme
2 bay leaves
½ head fennel, sliced, or celery, chopped
4 oz (100 g) dried chestnuts, soaked for 4 hours
8 oz (225 g) button mushrooms
1 large beefsteak tomato, chopped
1 tablespoon soft dark brown sugar
1½ teaspoons salt
Freshly ground black pepper
3 tablespoons fresh wholemeal breadcrumbs

Drain the haricot beans, then put in a large saucepan or flameproof
casserole. Add the olive oil, tomato purée, onion, garlic, herbs and
bay leaves, with water to cover. Stir and cook for 2½ hours over
very low heat or in a 350°F (180°C), gas mark 4, oven. (It is important *not* to add any salt at this stage as salt affects the cooking of the
beans.)

Remove from the heat and discard the onion. Add the fennel,
drained chestnuts, button mushrooms, tomato, sugar, salt and
pepper to taste. Sprinkle with the breadcrumbs and continue cooking in the oven at 350°F (180°C), gas mark 4, for 1 hour. Serve with a
green salad.

VEGETARIAN COUSCOUS
Serves 4–6

In countries where meat is scarce, or for religious reasons is not eaten, vegetarian dishes are the norm and not just adapted from meat dishes using other ingredients as substitutes. So, in North Africa, all along the coast, there are various versions of a dish called couscous. It's made from tiny pieces of semolina rolled in flour, then steamed over savoury broths in which meat and/or vegetables, sometimes even fish, are cooked. The grains are served with the meat, vegetables or fish mixed in, moistened with the broth and seasoned with a fiery, vicious sauce called *harissa*. I give the recipe but it ought to carry a government health warning – 'This sauce can damage your mouth'.

Different towns, different families and, especially, different countries use different ingredients for their sauces and broths for couscous. This version is traditional in Algeria, although some of the vegetables have been substituted for things we can find more easily in Britain. Although it originates in a hot country it's a very warming dish for our much colder climate, and makes a marvellous party centrepiece. It can be made in large quantities without too much effort or expense. There is authentic equipment but the method I describe below – using a saucepan and a colander – will do just as well.

6 oz (175 g) chick-peas,
soaked for 4 hours, drained and boiled for 1 hour
1 lb (450 g) onions
8 oz (225 g) each carrots, green beans, courgettes and tomatoes, chopped
1 clove garlic, crushed
1 teaspoon turmeric
1 teaspoon each salt and freshly ground black pepper
1 lb (450 g) couscous
(this can be bought in health food shops, usually pre-cooked)
2 fl oz (50 ml) olive oil
½ pint (300 ml) warm water

Harissa
2 cloves garlic
1 teaspoon chilli powder
½ teaspoon ground cumin

Choose a large saucepan into which a colander (or sieve) will fit comfortably, leaving at least 6 inches (15 cm) underneath. Put the chick-peas, onions, carrots, green beans, courgettes, tomatoes, garlic, turmeric and salt and pepper into the saucepan. Cover with at least 2 inches (5 cm) water. If you want a very rich dish, fry the onions and garlic first for 3 or 4 minutes in a little oil, then add the other vegetables. Put the colander on top. In a separate bowl, stir the couscous with the olive oil and warm water; the couscous will absorb the water remarkably easily and start to swell up. Keep stirring it so it doesn't go lumpy but forms a smooth mixture, then pour into the colander. (Don't worry, it won't fall through the holes.) Put the saucepan and colander over a fairly high heat until the vegetable mixture boils, then put a tightly-fitting lid or tea towel over the top and steam for 30 minutes, until the couscous is thoroughly hot.

Take the couscous out of the colander and stir in another 8 fl oz (225 ml) warm water, which it will again absorb. Return to the colander and steam for another 10 minutes. (The couscous should now be the size of rice grains.) To serve, put the couscous in a large pile on a serving dish and make a big well in the middle. Place the various vegetables in the well and moisten the couscous with some of the broth.

To make the harissa, mix 8 fl oz (225 ml) of the stock with the garlic, the chilli powder and the cumin in a blender or food processor until thoroughly smooth. Serve in a separate bowl.

To eat, you take a portion of the couscous, a selection of vegetables, a pinch of harissa and enough stock to moisten it to your taste. Some people like eating it very runny like a soup, others very dry. Either way it's an amazing combination of richness and delicacy.

SAVOURY DUTCH PANCAKES
Serves 4

If you always thought pancakes were meant to be thin, lacy little things (like French crêpes or our slightly more solid arrangements for Shrove Tuesday), this pancake will dispel those illusions. Holland thinks of itself as the home of pancakes and they have a huge variety. This kind is eaten very much like pizza in Italy, or a tortilla in Spain, as a meal cooked on its own and in its own right. The method is very simple. The tricky bit is getting the batter to the right consistency, and this is affected very much by the type of flour you use because some absorb more water than others. I've suggested a volume of liquid (you can, by the way, use milk as well for extra richness), but you may find a little less or a little more will make proper 'single cream' consistency for the batter before you leave it to rest. You can also use one of the wholemeal flours in this recipe if you want a little more fibre in your diet, but that's not traditional in Holland. To serve, cut the pancake in wedges like a cake and have a green salad waiting to follow. It's surprisingly solid and filling.

6 oz (175 g) plain flour
2 eggs
1 teaspoon vegetable oil
Approximately ½ pint (300 ml) water or milk to make a creamy consistency
1 shallot or small onion, chopped
1 tablespoon each; vegetable oil and butter for frying
4 oz (100 g) mushrooms, sliced
4 oz (100 g) frozen peas
4 oz (100 g) Gouda cheese, diced
1 small green or red pepper, cored, seeded and chopped
Salt and freshly ground black pepper

To make the batter, mix the flour, eggs and oil together, then beat in the water or milk to make a 'single cream' consistency. Set aside to rest for 30 minutes.

Fry the shallot or small onion in a pan with the oil and butter for 2 minutes. Add the batter to the pan, let it cook for 1 minute, then add the mushrooms, peas, cheese and green or red pepper. Press into the batter, season, cover and gently cook for 6 minutes, until the batter is set. You can grill the top under a hot grill for 2 minutes, if you prefer.

The next four recipes were designed as accompaniments to roast lamb but, in fact, they make delicious vegetable dishes in their own right. I very often serve a range of four or five vegetable dishes like these as a meal on their own, without bothering with any meat. I've rarely known anybody complain.

POTATO, CELERIAC AND JERUSALEM ARTICHOKE PURÉE
Serves 4–6

I first had this purée many years ago in an incredibly expensive restaurant, specialising in exotic food. Celeriac and Jerusalem artichokes were new to me then, as well as to the majority of British people. Fortunately, both in the shops and garden catalogues, they are now easily available. Jerusalem artichokes look like knobbly potatoes, but have a slightly 'hazelnutty' flavour. Celeriac is a large round turnip-shaped vegetable that is a root-growing form of celery, with almost exactly the same flavour but with a much less stringy texture. You can serve this purée instead of mashed potatoes on almost any occasion, but it's particularly good with rich meats like game. You have to peel the celeriac, by the way, but the artichokes can get away with a good scrub.

1 lb (450 g) potatoes, peeled and diced into 1-inch (2.5-cm) cubes
8 oz (225 g) celeriac, peeled and diced into 1-inch (2.5-cm) cubes
8 oz (225 g) Jerusalem artichokes, scrubbed and diced into
1-inch (2.5-cm) cubes
5 tablespoons hot milk
Salt and freshly ground black pepper
Chopped fresh parsley (optional)

Boil the vegetables together for 20 minutes, then drain and mash thoroughly with hot milk. Season generously and serve hot. Chopped parsley is a fine addition to this dish.

CARROT AND SWEDE PURÉE
Serves 4–6
This is another vegetable purée, representing a trend in vegetable presentation that is enormously fashionable in France. This particular recipe, however, came from my Welsh childhood, where it was known as 'punchnep' and often made with turnips and/or parsnips as an alternative to the carrots or swede. It was roughly puréed and sometimes now, especially when I'm serving it with other suitable dishes, I don't get the purée absolutely smooth – I leave it with a little texture as it was in my childhood. Either way, what benefits this purée particularly, is a good deal of freshly ground black pepper. Don't be too mean with the butter as it contributes not only smoothness, but flavour.

1 lb (450 g) each carrots and swede, peeled and diced
2 tablespoons butter
Salt and freshly ground black pepper

Boil the carrots and swede for about 15 minutes, until tender. Drain very well and purée or mash the vegetables until fairly smooth. (A food processor is ideal but a sieve will do.) Add butter and season generously, especially with black pepper.

LEEKS IN WHITE SAUCE

Serves 4

One of the many vegetables that were ruined for me in school were leeks, cooked in white sauce. When cooked until they're khaki-coloured they can be absolutely atrocious. But if you cook the leeks gently and make the white sauce carefully it can be one of the most delicious of dishes. In Anglesey in North Wales they make the mixture slightly runnier than I suggest here. They add a little more milk to the white sauce, and then pour it over halved hard-boiled eggs and bake briefly in the oven. It is called Anglesey eggs and is a smashing supper dish.

Be careful when cleaning the leeks: they are almost always very gritty with lots of sand and dirt trapped inside their folds. If you fill a bowl with water and wash the leeks after they've been cut up into 1-inch (2.5-cm) pieces, you'll find you get more of the grit out more easily. Also, don't be tempted to cook them for more than 3 minutes, or the colour will make you think you're back at school, or worse – in the army.

1 tablespoon cornflour
1 tablespoon butter
½ pint (300 ml) milk
1 lb (450 g) leeks, cut into 1-inch (2.5-cm) pieces and washed
½ teaspoon grated nutmeg
Salt and freshly ground black pepper

To make the white sauce, whisk the cornflour, butter and milk together with a wire whisk, then heat to boiling, whisking constantly. Simmer for 3 minutes, and remove from the heat.

Blanch the leeks for 3 minutes in boiling water, then drain well. Add to the white sauce and stir, coating the leeks with the sauce. Add nutmeg and seasoning before serving. Serve hot.

ROAST PARSNIPS

Serves 6

Roast parsnips seem to be everybody's favourite. In fact, rather like prawns, I find they are one thing I never have enough of. The method of roasting them is, in fact, very similar to the right way to get perfect roast potatoes and involves a little parboiling first. This ensures the insides are cooked soft before the outsides are baked hard so that the pleasure of eating them is not replaced by the problem of getting into them. Be careful about the timing and make sure when you cut up the parsnips that they have a reasonable amount of bulk; they're not meant to be as thin as chips. If you have tiny parsnips leave them whole: they cook perfectly well this way.

1½ lb (700 g) parsnips, peeled and cut lengthways
4 tablespoons vegetable oil

Parboil the parsnips for 8 minutes, then drain carefully. Place on a hot baking tray with the oil pre-heated in it. Roll the parsnips in the oil and bake for 30 minutes at 350°F (180°C), gas mark 4, turning them at least once.

CLASSIC CABBAGE
Serves 4–6

That other school 'horror' – boiled cabbage – is, when cooked properly, one of the most delicious vegetables I have ever eaten. You can use most kinds of cabbage, although I find that the very hard white Dutch cabbage, often used for coleslaw, isn't good when used for this recipe; it lacks in flavour what it achieves in crispness. A round, or point-headed, cabbage, or one of the winter savoys, cooks beautifully by this method. Be careful not to overcook it – a couple of minutes too long sends you back to school just as surely as do overcooked leeks.

1½ lb (700 g) cabbage, washed
8 fl oz (225 ml) water
1 oz (25 g) butter
Salt and freshly ground black pepper

Just before you're ready to cook, trim and cut the cabbage into 1-inch (2.5-cm) ribbons, using a sharp knife. Mix the water and butter together in a saucepan big enough to take all the cabbage at once with a good tight-fitting lid. Bring to the boil, then add the cabbage and 1 teaspoon salt. Stir quickly over maximum heat, cover and leave for 1 minute. Give the pan a thorough shake, holding the lid on tightly with your other hand. Wait another 30 seconds, then serve. Season with freshly ground black pepper. The cabbage will be crisp, hot, aromatic and buttery. Don't let it sit around before you eat.

RED CABBAGE
Serves 6–8

Red cabbage is a vegetable we often eat pickled in this country. And very nice it is too, especially with a decent Lancashire hot-pot. In Europe, particularly eastern Europe, it's made into a vegetable casserole of its own with very sophisticated savoury flavours and a hint of sweetness that makes it ideal for eating with winter meats and particularly game (see Game, Goose and Offal, page 83).

1 tablespoon vegetable oil
(traditionally meat dripping is used)
2 lb (900 g) red cabbage, sliced into ½-inch (1-cm) ribbons
1 lb (450 g) cooking apples, cored and chopped
1 lb (450 g) onions, chopped
1 tablespoon malt vinegar
1 tablespoon brown sugar
½ teaspoon ground allspice
1 teaspoon salt
Generous pinch of freshly ground black pepper

Heat the oil in a large, heavy-based saucepan or flameproof casserole. Stir in the vegetables with the vinegar, sugar, allspice, salt and pepper and enough water just to cover. Bring to the boil, turn down to simmer, cover and cook for at least 45 minutes, until the cabbage is tender. It can be cooked for up to 1½ hours and is even better if left to cool, then re-heated the next day.

STEAMED CAULIFLOWER AND BROCCOLI WITH SESAME
Serves 4–6

These days the variety of broccolis and cauliflowers we can get is really quite interesting. Apart from the classic white cauliflower and bright green broccoli, which are widely available most of the year, a new cauliflower variety, which is really an old kind, has come on the market in some areas. It is pale, almost lime green and is what the bright white ones were developed from. It has a slightly more intense flavour and looks most attractive served with white cauliflower and broccoli.

For about 1½ to 2 months during the winter you can get all three vegetables; that's what I'm suggesting for this dish, which makes a lovely centrepiece for a vegetarian meal, or an interesting side dish for grilled or plainly cooked meats. It is particularly nice with Beef Teriyaki (see page 75). If you can find only one or two of the varieties of cauliflower, however, it works perfectly well with those – you just get a slightly less pretty dish with less variation of texture and flavour. The basic technique is Chinese, but you don't need to use a wok or chopsticks to have this for supper.

1½ lb (700 g) cauliflower and/or broccoli
and/or green cauliflower (see above), washed and broken
into 2-inch (5-cm) florets
Salt
1 tablespoonful good-quality soy sauce
2 oz (50 g) sesame seeds
1 dessertspoon sesame oil (optional – available in the
Chinese and Indian sections of supermarkets and specialist shops)

Place the florets in a vegetable steamer with about 2½ inches (6 cm) water in the pan below. Bring the water to the boil and lightly salt the florets, then steam, covered, for just 8 minutes. When tender, remove to a serving dish and sprinkle with the soy sauce.

While the cauliflower is steaming, dry roast the sesame seeds very carefully in a small frying pan over a moderate heat; they should be pale gold in colour, but be careful not to let them burn or get the heat too high as they may pop. You can also toast them in the oven, if you wish. Sprinkle the toasted sesame seeds and soy sauce over the cauliflower and broccoli florets, arranged in colour groups if you are using more than one kind. Finally, sprinkle with delicious sesame oil.

Crafty steaming

The Chinese, who probably invented steaming, use a series of tiered baskets with open-work bottoms, balanced on top of a pot or wok filled with water. You can cook more than one layer of food at a time by this method. The baskets are widely available from Chinese shops and some specialist kitchen shops. If, however, you want a simple vegetable steamer, find a colander or sieve that fits tightly into a large saucepan, leaving at least 1 inch (2.5 cm) space between the top of the water and the bottom of the colander or sieve. Make sure the lid still fits over the top as this speeds up steaming considerably. Also ensure the colander or sieve is firm and stable when the food's cooking, so that it doesn't slip or slide dangerously. Using this method, any of the normal steaming recipes can be followed. If you have to put a dish inside the colander or sieve, arrange a safe method of getting it out again when it's hot – a piece of string or a folded strip of foil run under the plate with pieces hanging over the sides of the pan to act as handles is the best way.

SPAGHETTI MARROW
Serves 4

An unlikely name for an unlikely vegetable, this looks like a honeydew melon both in shape and colour. The inside has a very different texture indeed. When it's cooked it produces a lot of long thin strings with the flavour of courgettes and looking rather like spaghetti. It's available from mid-December, and makes a marvellous low-calorie version of a gratin. The vegetable does not have very much taste and, therefore, benefits from being seasoned or sauced.

1 spaghetti marrow, halved lengthways and seeded
1 tablespoon vegetable oil
Salt and freshly ground black pepper
About 2 oz (50 g) freshly grated Parmesan cheese
½ oz (15 g) butter

Boil both halves of the spaghetti marrow in a large covered pan for 40 minutes, until tender. Drain and fork up the strands of 'spaghetti'. Mix with the oil. Season highly. Spoon into a buttered gratin dish. Sprinkle with cheese according to taste and dot with flecks of butter. Place under a pre-heated hot grill for 3 to 4 minutes until the cheese has melted and is bubbling.

YOGHURT GUACAMOLE
Serves 4

Guacamole's literal meaning in Aztec, the ancient Mexican language, is 'avocado sauce'. That's what it is in its normal form – a purée of avocados and other vegetables eaten as a condiment with other dishes. My version uses yoghurt (see page 107 to make your own) and makes a very light starter to be eaten as a runny vegetable pâté. A few corn or tortilla chips, widely available made from natural and unadulterated ingredients, go very well with this.

8 oz (225 g) natural yoghurt
1 soft avocado, peeled
½ green pepper, cored, seeded and chopped
½ red pepper, cored, seeded and chopped
2 tomatoes, chopped
1 teaspoon lemon juice
1 teaspoon salt

Mash the avocado and add the other ingredients. Stir well and serve in cocktail glasses with crunchy savoury biscuits.

A FRESH LOOK AT WATER

ALTERNATIVES TO THE TAP

JILL GOOLDEN

If you're less than enthusiastic about your tap water, bottled water and water filters are good alternatives. But which brand and which make? Jill looks at the alternatives.

A New Age is poised ready to dawn on Britain, according to some experts – apparently we are about to enter the Third Age of Water. Or to put it another way, the Glorious Age of the Third Tap – that's how the companies spending millions on research into plumbed-in water filters like to see it, anyway. Market research has revealed some of us are so disillusioned with the state of tap water, we will soon be rushing off to buy a plumbed-in permanent filter to treat our drinking water ... that is the speculation at any rate.

There has been an unprecedented boom in the sale of bottled drinking waters. Sales – estimated at well over 100 million litres a year – have quadrupled this decade, and gone up an astonishing 25 times since the mid-seventies. This is despite the shattering reality that bottled water costs anything from 500 times more per glass than London tap water. And – even more shocking to me – this outstripped the cost per litre of petrol during much of this period of amazingly buoyant growth. As proof that we are ripe for an alternative, these statistics certainly hold water well.

I must say I have had my own doubts about tap water ever since I did a 'blind' water tasting on *Food and Drink*, to see whether I could tell one bottled water from another and whether they were noticeably different from good old tap water.

As I sat behind the drinks bar waiting for my turn, I gazed at the unmarked water carafes piercingly, willing them to give me some clue as to their identity. For once, the crystal ball technique paid off. I didn't suddenly see a genie rise up out of the bottle to reveal all, but what I *did* see was almost as helpful. I suddenly realised the water in one carafe was quite different in appearance from the others. Where they were quite bright and clear, this particular carafe was unfortunate enough to hold a yellow-tinged liquid, which certainly did not look entirely transparent. It was obviously the tap water. When I got round to tasting, it proved neither pleasant nor fresh.

I know talk of water 'recycling' is evocative and almost guaranteed to put you off any such water in the glass. But in the course of duty for *Food and Drink*, I rode on a revolving arm at a sewage treatment plant, and realised recycled water can be wholesome after all. Not much worse, when you think of it, than water 'recycled' by the clouds. So I can promise I haven't allowed my tasting judgement to be jaded by unpleasantly emotive thoughts. And I *still* don't like most tap waters very much, and am open to any suggestions of reasonable alternatives.

I claim no responsibility for prompting the dawning of this New Age of Water. That has been helped along by a recent *Which?* survey of British water. Apparently extensive research revealed one third of people polled were unhappy with their tap water. They complained it tasted poor, was discoloured, had 'bits' in it – and was rather offputting, not to mention fears it might be a health hazard.

According to *Which?*, almost one in four people in Britain may be drinking water that doesn't measure up to EEC standards. *Which?* states that 'The main pollutants, which vary from place to place are lead, which can damage the brain and nervous system; nitrates, which can increase the risk of blood disorders in bottle-fed babies; and aluminium, a suggested cause of senile dementia, as well as iron and manganese.'

Since we have to depend on the water supply we are given, this is a disquieting list, although there is some evidence that these *Which?* allegations may be rather sensational. But there is no question that the offending constituents do occur in water supplies throughout Britain, particularly in the south-west, Wales, the Midlands, East Anglia, the north-west, the north-east and Scotland, and in sufficient quantities not to measure up to EEC standards. You would, however, have to drink a great deal to take in enough of the pollutants for them to have an adverse effect.

A Water Authorities Association spokesman said: 'Items listed by *Which?* can be dangerous if consumed in large quantities, but none is present in the public supply in anything but minute amounts.' Minute, perhaps, but nitrate levels in the public water supply in some areas can be much higher than the limit set by the EEC and still be quite legal by the more relaxed British standards. Certainly the waters have been sufficiently muddied for seekers of alternatives (such as myself) to be viewed as quite normal rather than suggestible cranks.

The most easily accessible, affordable alternatives to unpleasant-tasting water from the tap are bottled waters and small home water filters in the form of jugs which 'adjust' the composition and taste of freshly run tap water. Since the Age of the Third Tap is still largely on the drawing board, plumbed-in units have not yet established themselves as a third serious option. There are some available at present, priced from £30, including several from Royal Doulton, a company involved in the development of water filters for more than 150 years.

In 1827, drinking water in Westminster, London, was officially described as 'offensive to sight, disgusting to the imagination and destructive to the health'. A company called Doulton and Watts experimented in making portable filter cases from glazed stoneware. Henry Doulton, aspiring heir to the company, was bribed by his father with a promise of a horse if he could come up with a perfect 3-gallon example, and, as the story goes, he managed to make 15 samples before breakfast, winning the horse. Today Royal Doulton make both plumbed-in filters and large free-standing ones, which they sell to more than 100 countries. It is a sign of the times that they are now selling quite a few of their models in Britain, too.

Not so very long ago bottled water was virtually unheard of in Britain. People on the Continent drank it because they had to; their own water supply was untrustworthy – or so we thought. At home, our water was whiter than white and we knew we were safe to drink it wherever we were. So we didn't really bother with bottles, except perhaps Malvern, occasionally offered as a pure partner for whisky.

The principal reason for buying bottled water in, say, France was that it was pollutant-free and safe. When the fashion swept over here, gradually the health angle gathered its own momentum as well. Where tap water comes from rivers, lakes and reservoirs, and is open to contamination from all manner of pollutants deriving from agriculture, industry and humans, bottled mineral and spring waters come from protected underground sources. The water filters through, and is cleaned by, the geological structure of the earth.

Some bottled waters taste very neutral and bland, while others have a powerful flavour of their own, derived from a cocktail of minerals picked up along the route through the earth and the rocks. Some are lightly mineralised, while others have a high mineral content and may not suit everyone. There were a couple of mineral waters from Europe that were actually banned in the United States for containing too much arsenic. The content was negligible, but it was there, and proved too much for the American health watchdogs.

The most popular bottled waters in Britain are only lightly mineralised, unlike some of the best-sellers in France. On the Continent, they seem to imagine that if it's unpleasant to taste, it must be doing you good. Happily that 'hair shirt' reasoning hasn't caught on here. As a straightforward alternative to the tap, still waters are preferred, although there is bigger business in those with bubbles, almost all artificially added by carbonation, as in lemonade.

One notable exception to the carbonation rule is Perrier, the best-seller, which emerges from the earth in its sparkling state. When the water is bottled, the CO_2 is collected and later reunited with the water, resulting in a fizzy water. Badoit also has a natural sparkle, but this is bottled along with the water, with no additional pumping. The result is a mildly sparkling water – it has only a faint prickle – coupled with a very individual sweet-and-astringent taste which, I think, makes it a delicious drink in its own right.

Of the 'bland' school, good examples are the deliciously fresh-tasting French Evian, which, it is estimated, takes 15 years to filter through the Alps from catchment to source, and Scotland's very lightly mineralised Highland Spring, which may be either still, as it emerges from the earth, or energetically carbonated. Sainsbury's Scottish Spring comes from an adjacent source and is identical in all respects but price – you get a considerable saving on the supermarkets' own brands of spring and mineral waters.

Jug water filters operate on your household water supply from the tap. They cost about £10 initially, and the filter must be replaced every month or so – or every 75–100 litres (130–175 pints) – at an additional cost of £1.75 to £2.75. To operate, fill the jug with tap water and wait for it to percolate through the filter to emerge transformed – and instantly usable for drinking or cooking.

The essential ingredient of the filter in all jugs is chemically activated carbon, which attracts certain chemicals and sediments and encourages them to stick on the carbon's surface. The filtered water emerges minus some discolouring solids, principally iron, chlorine and other organic compounds that give water its 'off' taste.

So far so good. But as with so many other apparent brainwaves, there are snags. Carbon itself, for instance, acts like a kind of propagator for bacteria; they love it. So, once the chlorine has been taken out of the water, bacterial growth can be a risk. To counteract this, the carbon may be treated with metallic silver, which is bacteriostatic ... but silver is a toxin and miniscule amounts may escape into the water.

Jug filters are definitely *not* suitable for treating possibly contaminated waters from rivers or wells or when you are travelling abroad. The *Which?* report maintains that 450,000 households use unregulated private supplies, and should therefore steer well clear of these jugs – a point not stressed in the various manufacturers' leaflets. Surprisingly there aren't any compulsory health and efficiency tests on water filters in the UK, so the various claims cannot be verified.

Some of the filters, for example, contain synthetic resins, designed to remove several 'hidden components', the components varying from filter to filter. It is claimed by the literature attached to one filter, for instance, that nitrates are taken out – but rival companies allege that even if they are, once the filter has filled up with the impurities, they simply spill back into the water in the jug later on.

Fed up with a chronic case of kettle scale (living in London, I found that a new kettle I bought was heavily scaled within two days of its christening), I decided to adopt a water filter as a fully integrated member of the household and resolved to use it consistently for drinking water, and for the kettle. And the kettle benefited immediately. But did my family?

I admit I was obviously an imperfect user. I have a fetish (perfectly well founded, I am assured by all water experts from the Water Board down) for freshly run water, so it was no use merely filling the jug and leaving it merrily to filter through until next I needed a glass or kettleful. I had to fill it each time and wait. This led to two obvious snags. The first was that waiting for the freshly run tap water to drip slowly through the gadget was about as time saving as drawing your own water from a well, and the second was that, between draughts, I occasionally allowed the filter to dry out.

The drying out is an unspeakable crime, because the contaminated carbon immediately begins to flake off and deposit itself in your next glass. But I persevered with a new filter, mended my ways and kept it permanently submerged. And still, after a time, began to notice a different – rather unpleasant – taste seeping through. It became clear the portable filter was not for me. If I am not bankrupted by buying too many bottles of mineral water in the meantime, perhaps I had better prepare myself instead for entry into the Age of the Third Tap.

Best of the water filters

Extensive taste testing of six of the available jug filters proved (to the satisfaction of our panel) that they do affect the taste of the water considerably ... but not always to its advantage.

Waterboy
Best liked, although it does impart a very distinctive minerally and sweet character to the water.

Filtaware
Produced a slightly chalky taste, and seemed to reduce the evidence of chlorine.

Leifheit
Chlorine noticeable after filtration in 'tinny' tasting water, very bright in appearance.

Mayrei
An inexpensive tap fitment that reduces tap water's 'off' flavours to produce a rather bland, dull taste.

Brita
Pioneer in the field, and pleasing design. Seems to give filtered water a rather metallic taste.

Weighmaster Crystal
Altered tap water most noticeably, giving it plasticy, 'milk of magnesia' alkaline flavours that you might not welcome.

BEEF, LAMB & HAM

INTRODUCTION
CHRIS KELLY

In which a master butcher reveals to Chris the secrets of British beef and a recipe for home-cooked ham triumphs over the packaged variety.

'Things got so desperate, we were asking scientists if they could breed six-legged sheep!' Ken Clements says, reminiscing about rationing, when the hardest thing about butchering was pleasing the customer, and fiddles were rife. There was the time, he remembers, when a local shop had just taken delivery of a load of 'knocked off' meat. Suddenly, with a sadistic sense of occasion, a pair of large feet and a trenchcoat – the dreaded supervisor – appeared on the scene. 'Ah, Mr Cornish,' said the butcher, demonstrating a commendable flair for improvisation, 'I was just about to get on the blower to you. I think they've sent the wrong meat.' The stern Mr Cornish, however, was not to be persuaded, still less bribed with a pork chop.

Born into a family of butchers in 1916 – his grandfather was one of the first traders in London to sell New Zealand lamb – Ken Clements remembers his introduction to Smithfield Market at the age of eight. His father parked the car (the horseless carriage was still a relative novelty) opposite the Old Bailey, where a firm of carriers had their stables. Ken has never forgotten a nearby pub, the Magpie and Stump, whose upper room, he was told, had once been hired out to spectators at public executions. At Smithfield everyone knew his Dad – 'Got the guvnor with you?' – and the bustling excitement of the place made a lasting impression, as seemingly endless queues of horse-drawn wagons hauled meat up the slope from the market's own underground goods station, now a vast car park.

An only child, Ken went into the business as a matter of course, and stayed in it, interrupted only by the War, until the 1970s. Then he was asked by the Inner London Education Authority to become a full-time lecturer at Smithfield College, a faculty of the College for Distributive Trades, teaching students about meat, including breeding, feeding, slaughtering, refrigeration, cutting and preparation, as well as business management. He served as Chairman of the Institute of Meat, and is still Treasurer of the London Meat Traders' Association, as well as being a Freeman of the City of London and a Liveryman of the Worshipful Company of Butchers. In short, Ken Clements, my guide to the modern Smithfield, knows a bit about meat.

Eighteen stone and jovial, with a vigorous moustache, horn-rimmed spectacles and dark, bushy eyebrows, Ken deserves to be called the 'Baron of Beef'. All the market traders know him, just as they knew his father – 'Good morning, Mr Clements, Sir' – the 'Sir' delivered with affection and respect. Striding down the central aisle, between the hanging carcasses, he pulls no punches. 'Now there's a bit of rubbishy meat,' he says, seeing a haunch of beef, as tough and muscular as a weight-lifter's thigh. 'No marbling, no covering – very little to recommend it at all.' Similarly, a consignment of lamb, whose leanness and lack of subcutaneous fat tells him that it has been crossed with Continental varieties, earns his scorn.

What are the main changes Ken has seen in Smithfield over 60 years? Two, he says. Now, because consumers are more specific about what they want, butchers increasingly come to the market looking for main cuts, rather than whole carcasses. Also fewer butchers come because more and more are buying direct from abattoirs, where meat is processed into main cuts, vacuum packed and boxed after slaughter. This is possibly a long-term threat to the market as a whole.

Finally, we reach the aristocrats of the beef world – the mature carcasses from Scotland, with their overcoat of pale creamy yellow fat and their deep, bright 'shining' red meat. (Rumour has it that formerly some Irish beef was imported and sold as Scottish, probably on the grounds it had Angus or Galloway antecedents. The cattle would be shipped, live, to Stranraer and fattened there for six months, before being slaughtered and sent across the border to pose as something they weren't. Now, however, the 'Scottish Quality Beef' mark, or label, is a guarantee that the meat is genuinely born and bred in Scotland.) What is it, exactly, that sets Scottish beef above the rest, making it worth a premium?

To begin with, the breeding stock is second to none. Aberdeen Angus and Galloway, the two main breeds, are particularly good at producing mature carcasses with the right balance of subcutaneous fat and well-developed intra-muscular fat, sometimes called 'marbling'. During cooking this effectively allows the meat to baste from the inside; one of the qualities which make Angus, a small breed, so suitable for crossing. Secondly, in summer, Scottish beef cattle are grass-fed rather than grain-fed (though the lushness of Scottish meadows is as indefinable an ingredient as is the pure water which makes Scotch whisky inimitable). Importantly as well, Scottish beef is slaughtered at 18 to 20 months, as opposed to the untimely death suffered by intensively reared cattle at 10 to 12 months; the younger the animal, the less developed its flavour.

On specific cuts of beef, Ken has the following advice to offer:
Topside Always safer to pot roast, or roast in tinfoil, to retain the steam, which tenderises. Finish for the last 15 minutes or so in an open oven, to brown.
Silverside Suitable for braising, pot roasting or salting; the muscle structure is too coarse to make it a satisfactory roasting joint.
Sirloin Can be cooked in an open oven with no special treatment; usually has more fat, which makes it crisper.
Fore-rib The unanimous choice of a *Food and Drink* tasting panel (including Michael Barry, Jocelyn Dimbleby and Ken Clements – see Michael's recipe that follows). Can be cooked on or off the bone but Ken favours on for three reasons:
1 The bone conducts the heat into the 'eye' of the meat, so it cooks inside as well as outside.
2 The meat shrinks less than it would if the bone were removed.
3 The marrow will cook out of the bone, enhancing the flavour.

Passing on to home-grown lamb, among the most seasonal of meats, the best time to buy is in the autumn, when supplies are plentiful. Asked which region produces the finest, Ken diplomatically replied that it depends which region you come from. The Welsh claim their lamb is peerless, while the Lowland Scots tell you theirs makes the rest taste like mutton. Michael Barry insists that lamb from Romney Marsh in his adoptive county, Kent, is supreme because it feeds on fragrant herbs, but West Countrymen and women know otherwise. In truth, there's little to choose between them; they're all delicious.

Wherever the lamb originates, the most economical way to buy it, if you can possibly afford to, is in whole sides. Failing that, Ken suggests trying these less popular cuts:

The neck Good for stews and neck fillets for kebabs and even mince.

The breast A bit fatty, but tasty boned, rolled and stuffed.

The shoulder Regarded by some as the sweetest meat, but difficult to carve because of the blade bone. The way to deal with that is to run a sharp knife each side of it before the joint goes in the oven. The meat then cooks away from the bone, so when you take it out you can simply twist the shoulder blade (using a cloth or foil), and, in theory anyway, it should detach easily. Having spent some time with Ken, I would tend to trust his theories.

Ken and I wound up our morning at Smithfield with a look at St Bartholomew the Great, the only London church to survive the Great Fire intact; it was saved by being outside the city wall. Founded in 1123, it had a prior in the next century appropriately named John Bacun. I'm not in the habit of discussing the Big Questions before breakfast, but somehow, in conversation with the present incumbent, we touched on the after-life. 'I hope to go down,' he volunteered, 'I hear the standard of Bridge is better there.'

Wisely busying itself with more temporal concerns, *Food and Drink* recruited a Townswomen's Guild from the Birmingham area to do some objective research into ham. We suspected that home-cooked gammon, which is so simple to prepare, not only has a better flavour than the pre-cooked variety (some of which contains added water) but also compares favourably on price. In a blind tasting, the ladies of the Guild proved us right on both counts.

Many people buy pre-cooked ham in slices, and with home-cooked gammon there's a considerable shrinkage. In the interests of fair play, we broke down costs to reflect these considerations. The figures in brackets, therefore, represent the price per ¼ lb (100 g) cooked weight. The ham joints tasted were:

Home-cooked	**Pre-cooked**
Top-quality prime gammon (80p)	Roast ham, with no added water (£1)
Gammon slipper (55p)	Prime ham in packets (68p)
Shoulder of ham (40p)	Ham-cured shoulder (56p)

It's immediately apparent that, after cooking, home-prepared hams offer considerably better value than the commercially processed equivalents. Those who argue that the relatively high price of pre-cooked ham reflects the fact that it saves on labour obviously haven't given much thought to the minimal effort involved in boiling a ham:

1 Soak overnight, though some butchers say this is no longer necessary.

2 Put in a large pan, cover with water, and add a carrot, a couple of bay leaves and an onion stuck with cloves. Slowly bring to the boil.

3 Cover, reduce the heat and cook at a slow simmer for 25 minutes per lb (450 g), plus an extra 25 minutes for good luck.

4 Cool, then peel off the skin and serve.

If you prefer your ham baked or roasted, simmer for half the cooking time, then wrap the joint in foil and cook in the centre of a pre-heated oven at 350°F (180°C), gas mark 4, for the remainder of the cooking time. Half an hour before it's due to finish cooking, take off the foil and remove the skin. Score the fat in a diamond pattern and stick in cloves at the intersections for extra flavour. Cover with a glaze; this may consist of many or few ingredients, according to taste. The one used in the programme was:

1 tablespoon made mustard
1 tablespoon soft dark brown sugar
2 tablespoons toasted breadcrumbs
1 teaspoon toasted cinnamon (a cinnamon stick toasted and ground to powder will give a better flavour than the ready-ground variety)
Rind and juice of 2 oranges

Finally, return the joint to the oven and roast at 425°F (220°C), gas mark 7, for the last 30 minutes.

In summary, home-cooked ham took three of the top four places in the Birmingham ladies' tasting, scoring highest for both taste and price. It is a simple, delicious, neglected dish which is long overdue for a comeback.

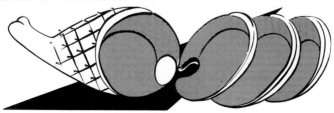

RECIPES
MICHAEL BARRY

ROAST BEEF

To roast a joint of beef successfully, whatever cut it is, only three things are essential. First know how much the beef weighs, second have an oven that's hot enough to begin with and third, allow the standing time at the end of the roasting period.

Given a choice of joints, I would choose fore-rib, for which knowledge I am indebted to Jocelyn Dimbleby and her view is confirmed by all the butchers I've talked to. It's often the joint they keep for themselves because we, the customers, don't know enough to ask for it. One other key thing about beef to roast is that it's worth buying a large joint. It's much more economical for a number of reasons, not the least being that you get much less shrinkage with a large joint. You have a much greater volume to surface area ratio and this means that you lose less beef in the roasting process, as all meat shrinks as it cooks. Also, you are almost certain to get better texture, moistness and flavour.

Never try roasting a piece weighing less than about 2½ lb (1.1 kg) by this method, otherwise you're likely to end up with no more than a shrivelled lump. Above that size, allow 12 minutes per 1 lb (450 g) for cooking and another 7 minutes per 1 lb (450 g) for standing afterwards. Standing should be in a warm place, but not the oven. It's crucial and prevents the meat being rubbery when you eat it. The cooking process goes on after the meat's taken out of the oven and it gives a chance for the juices to be re-absorbed. The meat tenderises itself and becomes far more succulent.

Lastly, for me the greatest virtue of roast beef is that it's as least as good cold as it is hot, so it's not just left-overs you're left with, but another complete meal.

Pre-heat your oven to 425°F (220°C), gas mark 7. Give it time to get thoroughly hot at this temperature, then place the beef on a rack in a roasting tin and put it in the oven on a middle shelf. Immediately turn the oven down to 350°F (180°C), gas mark 4, and allow the temperature to fall with the meat roasting in the oven. The intense high temperature at the beginning seals the meat, preventing loss of juices or flavour, and the declining temperature allows it to cook

SKATE IN BLACK BUTTER – PAGE 34

VEGETARIAN CASSOULET – PAGE 42

COLD BEEF PARISIENNE – PAGE 73

OXTAIL CASSEROLE – PAGE 89

APPLE CLAFOUTIS – PAGE 104

SWEET AND SOUR FISH WITH EXOTIC STIR-FRY – PAGE 122

CHICKEN FRICASSÉE
WITH RICE AND PEAS – PAGE 126

APRICOT JALOUSIE – PAGE 142

without burning. The 12 minutes per 1 lb (450 g) I recommend will produce rare roast beef. If you like your meat slightly better done, medium rare, allow 14 to 15 minutes per 1 lb (450 g), and if you like it pretty well done, allow 17 minutes. More than that, and you'd probably be better off braising the joint, because it will start drying out irretrievably. When the time is up, take it out of the oven and leave it to stand in a warm place for 7 minutes per 1 lb (450 g), whatever the length of time you've cooked it. Carve it across the grain for maximum succulence and texture.

HORSERADISH CREAM SAUCE FOR HOT ROAST BEEF
Makes about 6 oz (175 g)

This is the traditional sauce to go with beef in Britain alongside mustard, but it's too often ignored because it's badly made. At its best it can have a very delicate flavour, not overwhelming the beef in any way.

1 oz (25 g) fresh horseradish (this looks like a small parsnip), grated,
or ½ oz (15 g) dried horseradish
1 tablespoon lemon juice
1 teaspoon caster sugar
1 × 5 fl oz (150 ml) carton whipping cream

Finely grate the fresh horseradish, if using, taking care as you do so because it's pretty fiery stuff. If you're using the dried horseradish, re-hydrate it with just enough water to cover and leave for 10 minutes, then drain. Make sure that the bits of horseradish are really finely ground and if you're using dried you may find it useful to stick it in a blender or food processor just to make sure it's a smooth purée. Mix the horseradish with the lemon juice and sugar, then let stand for 5 minutes. Whip the cream until it's thick, but not stiff, and fold in the horseradish mixture. Leave the sauce to stand for at least 1 hour before using. It can be put in a sealed jar and kept in the fridge for up to 1 week. The fresh horseradish root, wrapped in cling film, will keep in the bottom of the fridge for a couple of weeks ready for the next time you want to use it.

COLD BEEF PARISIENNE
This is a classic French recipe for beef that's been cooked *à la mode*, but I think it's terrific with cold roast beef. It's using meat as a

salad *ingredient* in a way that's done on the Continent, whereas we merely use it as an adjunct to salad. I think this is best eaten with really top-class baked potatoes and one of the slightly bitter salads – endive, red chicory or the frissé that are, thankfully, widely available these days.

> 1 bunch spring onions
> 1 handful fresh parsley sprigs
> ½ teaspoon caster sugar
> ½ teaspoon each salt and freshly ground black pepper
> 1 teaspoon Dijon mustard
> 1 tablespoon cider vinegar
> 1 tablespoon lemon juice
> 6 tablespoons olive or salad oil
> Radish roses, tomato and cucumber slices, to garnish (optional)

Wash and trim the spring onions and parsley thoroughly. Cut the green bits off the onions and, with the parsley, chop as finely as possible; you can do this in a food processor or blender if you wish. Slice the white ends of the onions into very thin rings and then mix together with all the other ingredients, starting with the sugar, salt, pepper and mustard, then adding the vinegar and lemon juice, followed by the oil, and finally the parsley with the finely chopped green parts of the spring onions. Leave to stand for about 15 minutes so the flavours blend properly.

Take your slices of cold roast beef and spread them out on a large serving plate, so they don't overlap. They can be cut reasonably thickly, but shouldn't be in slabs! Spread the herb dressing over them and leave to marinate for at least 1 hour in the fridge. Garnish the edges of the plate and the centre of the meat too, if you like, with radish roses or sliced tomatoes and cucumber, and serve while still chilled.

THE GREAT BRITISH BRAISED BEEF
Serves 6

Topside is too dry to make a really superb roasting joint, but it is without question the best of all choices for roasting's first cousin – braising. The French make a great thing about 'braisés', but they are just as traditional on this side of the Channel. The perfect solution to a family who doesn't like its beef pink, but does like it moist, is a pot roast.

This recipe can be adapted to other cuts . . . the aitch bone best among them, but topside, with its leanness and its easily sliced shape, is ideal. Mustard, the traditional flavour with beef, is built into this version to add a tang that complements the succulence exactly.

3 lb (1.4 kg) rolled topside
2 tablespoons plain flour
Ground bay leaves and paprika (optional)
2 tablespoons vegetable oil
8 oz (225 g) carrots, peeled and coarsely chopped
8 oz (225 g) onions, coarsely chopped
½ pint (300 ml) water
1 teaspoon made English mustard
Salt and freshly ground black pepper

Heat a flameproof casserole (just large enough to hold the beef) until very hot. Rub the beef with the flour, which can have a pinch each of ground bay leaves and paprika in it. Pour the oil into the hot casserole and brown the meat quickly on all sides, then set aside. Brown the vegetables for 1 minute in the oil. Place the beef on top, stir the water and mustard together and pour over. Season well, cover and cook at 325°F (170°C), gas mark 3, for 1½ hours, until tender. Serve sliced with the juices and vegetables puréed together (for a sophisticated version) or as they come for a little rustic vigour.

BEEF TERIYAKI
Teriyaki is the name the Japanese give to a special soy sauce they make, used for coating fish and meat before grilling. Even Japanese housewives buy it ready-made these days. However, for crafty purists I give a basic recipe for Teriyaki Sauce below. You can use it whether you can find the ready-made article or not. The meat for this needs to be really tender. The famous *kobe* beef of Japan is reputed to be hand massaged every day to keep the cattle as tender as possible, so that when they are slaughtered the meat is cuttable with chopsticks. I don't know whether it's true or not, but I hope one day to go to find out personally.

The sauce is also used for chicken breasts that have been boned and skinned and, particularly, for fish steaks, notably salmon and tuna, which the Japanese are very fond of. In fact, Teriyaki makes a very good barbeque or grilling sauce for most things and can liven up a mid-week hamburger quite remarkably.

6–8 oz (175–225 g) sirloin steak per person
2 tablespoons Teriyaki Sauce per steak (see below)
1 teaspoon lemon juice per steak
Salad oil for grilling

Teriyaki Sauce
6 fl oz (175 ml) shoyu sauce (Japanese soy)
1½ oz (40 g) soft brown sugar
1 tablespoon cider vinegar
Pinch of ground ginger
Pinch of garlic powder, or 1 clove garlic, crushed

To make the sauce, mix all the ingredients together, carefully ensuring the sugar is dissolved in the shoyu sauce; this may take up to 2 hours and will need shaking carefully. The mixture should be slightly thicker than ordinary soy sauce and have a sour-sweet flavour, which is perfect for setting off meats.

Put the steaks in a shallow dish and brush all over with the Teriyaki Sauce, then set aside to marinate for at least 1 hour, turning during the period. It can be left for up to 4 hours, but not much longer than that. Before grilling, squeeze the lemon juice into the sauce mixture and give a final basting before placing on a very hot pre-heated grill, brushed with a little salad oil to help prevent sticking.

Grill the steaks for 2½–3 minutes each side: they should be slightly pink in the middle, but Japanese Beef Teriyaki is traditionally not eaten very rare. You can eat them like ordinary steaks with a knife and fork, but the Japanese would slice ¼-inch (0.5-cm) thick strips on the diagonal across the grain, before serving with rice and a salad made from raw grated carrot and radishes.

ROAST LAMB

We're pretty good at roasting lamb here in Britain and we certainly produce some of the best lamb in the world. But a lot of our top-quality produce goes abroad, to France in particular, where they know a thing or two about roasting lamb as well. This recipe is really French-derived in its flavours of rosemary and garlic, but the method is particularly crafty, as it has three special virtues apart from producing delicious roast lamb: it keeps the lamb particularly succulent and moist while it cooks; it makes the gravy automatically, and it makes the washing-up effortless as there are none of those nasty ground-in, baked-on hard bits to prise out of the roasting pan afterwards. The technique also makes sure the flavour of the herbs penetrates the meat, but doesn't overpower it.

Don't forget to allow the meat to stand after roasting to re-absorb its own juices and become really tender and moist. Use the same method for a shoulder of lamb, either with the bone in, or, if you can persuade your butcher to prepare it, boned and rolled, the way the French like it. If you're doing a shoulder, cook it for slightly fewer minutes per 1 lb (450 g), as it's normally not as bulky as a leg and will cook through more quickly.

2 cloves garlic
Salt
Vegetable oil
1 leg of lamb
½ pint (300 ml) water
1 tablespoon dried rosemary, or 2 large sprigs fresh rosemary

Crush the garlic cloves with some salt and a little oil. Spread this paste over the top of the lamb as if spreading butter. Place on a wire rack and set on top of a roasting pan containing the water. Sprinkle the dried rosemary or arrange the fresh rosemary around the sides of the lamb. Cook for 20 minutes per 1 lb (450 g) at 375°F (190°C), gas mark 5 (18 minutes per 1 lb (450 g) if using shoulder). Leave to stand for 5 minutes per 1 lb (450 g) in a warm place before carving. The cooking juices can form the basis of a great gravy.

LAVER SAUCE FOR ROAST LAMB

Laver is a form of seaweed known and eaten in a surprising number of parts of the world, from Ireland to Japan. It's a valuable source of vitamins, minerals and flavour. The most popular use in Britain these days is in South Wales, where it's mixed with oatmeal and made into cakes fried at breakfast time. In the eighteenth century, however, it was widely used all over Britain, particularly as a sauce for lamb and mutton. I think you will find it's both delicious and distinctive. It's sold as laver *bread* though there's no bread in it.

1 oz (25 g) butter
8 oz (225 g) prepared laver bread
(laver bread is normally always sold ready prepared)
Finely grated rind and juice of 1 orange
(use organic oranges if you wish to avoid fungicide wax on the skin)
Pinch of grated nutmeg

Melt the butter in a small, non-stick pan. Add the laver bread and heat through gently, then add the orange rind and juice and stir until smoothly blended. The sauce will be the colour of spinach and slightly shiny. Stir in the nutmeg and serve hot with the roast lamb, using it like a gravy, rather than a condiment like mustard.

PROVENÇALE SAUCE FOR ROAST LAMB

The rosemary and garlic flavourings I suggest for the roast leg of lamb are really Provençale in combination. This sauce is a version of ratatouille, the Provence vegetable stew, transformed into a sauce to go with and enrich roast lamb. Around Nice it's often eaten with *macaroniade*, fairly thick pasta tubes sauced with the lamb juices instead of potatoes as an accompaniment.

This sauce is equally nice cold with cold meats. Add a small handful of black olives, preferably stoned, in the last 5 minutes of cooking for a really true Niçoise flavour.

8 oz (225 g) aubergine, unpeeled and cut into ½-inch (1-cm) dice
Salt and freshly ground pepper
2 tablespoons olive oil
1 large Spanish onion, finely chopped
2 cloves garlic, finely chopped
2 ripe tomatoes, cut into ½-inch (1-cm) dice
1 tablespoon thick tomato purée
½ teaspoon each dried oregano and basil

Sprinkle the aubergine with a couple of tablespoons of salt and leave for 20 minutes, to drain off its bitter juices. When the aubergine is ready, heat the oil in a large frying pan. Rinse the aubergine pieces to remove the salt, pat dry with kitchen paper and briskly fry for 2 minutes, then add the onion and garlic. Turn down the heat and simmer for 5 minutes. Add the tomatoes and the tomato purée, thinned to the consistency of double cream with a little water. Turn the heat right down, season with the herbs and some pepper, but be a bit careful about salt as the aubergines have had quite a lot on them already. Cook for 25–30 minutes, until all the vegetables are soft but just distinct. Serve hot with the sliced lamb.

APPLE JELLY

Of course, the customary accompaniment to roast lamb is a redcurrant or apple jelly, and Germaine Greer demonstrated this traditional recipe for us. Germaine Greer has in recent years been advocating some of the more traditional virtues of peasant societies. This recipe is typical of that attitude. It uses very simple, very old-fashioned techniques to make a lovely preserve that, at its best, is not only delicious eaten like a jam on bread, but is very valuable for saucing and enhancing meat and game dishes.

**A large amount of cooking apples, peeled, cored and sliced
(Germaine Greer used Howgate Wonder apples)
Caster sugar**

Put the apples into a large saucepan over a low heat, cover and cook until they have turned to mush. Spoon into a jelly bag hanging over a saucepan and allow to drip slowly, *without squeezing the bag.* This will take approximately 24 hours.

When all the juice has dripped into the saucepan, add an equal amount of caster sugar, then bring to the boil, stirring to prevent sticking.

To test if the mixture has set, put a spot of the apple jelly on to a plate to see if it runs. If it begins to form a skin it's all right. If the mixture hasn't set, keep on the boil, still stirring, for a bit longer. Spoon into warm sterilised jars, seal and cover.

NAVARIN OF LAMB
Serves 6–8
This stew was traditionally made in the spring (hence its French name – Navarin Printanier). The combination of lamb and vegetables is a delicious one. Some versions include new potatoes in the recipe as well, but I think they're best cooked separately, otherwise there's nothing to contrast the flavours against.

**2 lb (900 g) shoulder or boned breast of lamb,
cut into pieces 2 inches × ½ inch (5 cm × 1 cm)
8 oz (225 g) onions, cut into ½-inch (1-cm) slices
8 oz (225 g) carrots, cut into batons
8 oz (225 g) turnips, cut into batons
2 sticks celery, cut into ½-inch (1-cm) slices
8 oz (225 g) stringless green beans, topped and tailed and cut in half
lengthways
Pinch each of dried thyme and marjoram
Salt and freshly ground black pepper
1 tablespoon cornflour
1 tablespoon tomato purée**

In a sauté pan or flameproof casserole large enough to hold all the ingredients, put the lamb, fat side down. Over a gentle heat brown it in its own fat for about 5 minutes. Add the onions and stir, then add the root vegetables and the celery. Add enough water to come halfway up, cover and gently cook for 20 minutes, stirring occasionally. Check the liquid to make sure the dish is not drying out, then add the beans and a pinch of thyme and marjoram. Season generously and bring to a gentle boil, cover and cook for another 15 minutes. Mix the cornflour with about 8 fl oz (225 ml) water and the tomato purée until smooth. Dish the meat and vegetables into a serving dish with sides. Make the cooking juice up to about ½ pint (300 ml) with water, then add the tomato and cornflour mixture. Bring to the boil, stirring, until it thickens, then pour the sauce over the meat. The dish should be quite liquid – it's really a stew. Serve it with boiled new potatoes, which I wouldn't bother to peel but just scrub well. Eat them in their jackets.

D R I N K S
JILL GOOLDEN

SIMPLE GUIDE TO BUYING RED WINES

Red wines traditionally accompany red meats. But if you prefer lighter reds to the more full-bodied ones, or vice versa, how can you tell which is which – particularly when you are not allowed to taste before buying. What is needed is a classification like there is for white wines. But working it out is not that easy, as Jill explains.

The tongue is a very complex creature. In charge of the incredibly valuable job of deciphering and appreciating taste, the tongue has a very responsible role to play. And a tricky one, not least because, as I've written, apparently the taste buds inlaid into the tongue's surface can only detect four basic sensations: sweetness, sourness, bitterness and saltiness. From these the tongue formulates a kind of chemical equation to relay to the brain a single, memorable, individual taste.

Because the apparent dryness or sweetness of a white or rosé wine is one of the most immediately detectable taste components, not surprisingly they are much easier to put into pigeon holes than are reds, which are virtually all dry. None of the individual taste sensations can be used on its own to classify red wines. So although a simple guide classifying all the white wines on the supermarket or wine shop shelves was devised a while ago (see page 35), it took much longer for the combined buds of the wine trade to come up with a simple guide to classify reds.

Now there is a Red Wine Taste Guide which is gradually being adopted by supermarkets and wine shops which attempts to classify in terms of total taste. The taste sensations that contribute to a wine's placing on the A to E scale are: the weight of the wine (its body and apparent denseness); the concentration of flavour; the level of apparent tannin – that is the element derived from the skins of the grapes, and from the wood if the wine has been stored in oak barrels at all during its life – which affects the outside of the tongue a bit like lemon juice and gives the wine an astringently dry quality; and the level of alcohol. Combined together, these qualities enable the wines to be simply categorised.

A Signifies a light red wine, without much depth; it can be fruity and appealing, but not overpowering, and the tannic quality will be barely discernible.
B A wine with slightly more guts, fuller body and a richer flavour.
C The middle of the range, medium-bodied wine with rather more backbone, but not so much flavour and 'bite' as to overpower simple food.
D The category for the heavier wines, denser and more concentrated.
E The class of the real heavyweights: wines that really fill the mouth with complex flavours and have a terrific thwack of tongue-puckering tannin. These are generally the highest in alcohol and best match strong meats such as game (see the next chapter).

Here is how some well-known red wines (named after the place they come from, their official quality or the grape they're made from) fit into the scale:

A Bardolino, Beaujolais, EEC table wines, German red wines, Touraine wines and Spain's Valdepeñas.
B Beaujolais Villages and single village wines, Côtes-du-Roussillon, Merlot, Navarra, Pinot noir and red Burgundies, Saumur, Valencia, Valpolicella and French vins de pays.
C Bergerac, non-specific wines from Australia, New Zealand and Yugoslavia, Clarets, Corbières, Côtes-du-Rhône, Minervois, North African wines and Riojas.

D Bairrada, Cabernet Sauvignon, Châteauneuf-du-Pape, Chianti, Dão, Fitou, Hungarian reds and Syrah.

E Barolo, Crozes-Hermitage, Cyprus and Greek reds and Australian Shiraz.

GAME, GOOSE & OFFAL

INTRODUCTION
CHRIS KELLY

Chris believes that it's time to dispel the mystique that still lingers over the preparation and cooking of game, for too long the preserve of aristocratic tables.

'Twelve bores', 'plus fours', 'a brace of birds' – the mathematics of hunting and shooting sound almost as unfamiliar to most of us as the jargon of dentists. We know roughly what they mean but they somehow don't seem to belong to us. Game – whether fish, feather or fur – obstinately retains an image which is both largely inaccurate and unfortunate. Historical fact and fiction have combined to characterise the pursuers of game as rich, if not actually aristocratic, hunters, blasting away at anything from elephant (not all that plentiful in Leicestershire!) to partridge, just for the fun of the kill. As well as being full of plunging pheasants, the air has been thick with emotive and condemnatory phrases like 'ritual slaughter'. Whereas the French think nothing of seeing their compatriots shoot practically everything furry or feathery that moves, we mount our high horse at the first whiff of cordite. As games go, we seem to think, this one is distinctly ill-matched.

Bagging birds and animals for both sustenance and pleasure has been part of our national outdoor life for centuries. Hunting, as a sport, was given a leg-up by royalty, who preserved their stock so zealously that poaching on Crown land was punishable by deportation even as late as Victorian times. Today's fieldsportsman, however, is much more likely to be a farmer or enthusiast on a day off than a belted Earl. I deliberately didn't add 'or field-sportswoman' because women are still as rare in a line of guns as elephants are in Leicestershire.

I suspect the natural beauty of many game birds and animals has also counted against their acceptance as an everyday source of food. We think of the stag as too 'noble' and 'handsome' to end in slices on a plate, and yet have no such qualms about cattle. We consider it regrettable to kill a cock pheasant, and yet put to death billions of chickens. We're equally illogical about the *coup de grâce*. It's all right, apparently, to rear captive pigs intensively and then despatch them without ceremony, but unacceptable to end a mallard's freedom with a single shot.

Even when all our other misconceptions about game are laid to rest, many still need reassuring on the business of preparation. Plucking a partridge sounds unimaginably difficult but turns out to be perfectly simple. In any case, you're hardly likely to have to do it because game dealers, butchers and game shops supply birds oven-ready. Similarly, you can forget horror stories of pheasants left to hang until they turn green and erupt with maggots. Should you ever have to cope with it, the hanging process is a matter of common sense and personal preference.

By avoiding game from whatever motive, we're denying ourselves an extraordinary variety of delicious, healthy, nourishing and, in many cases, economical dishes. Raised naturally and relatively fat-free, game birds and animals have a great deal to recommend them. It would take a separate slim volume to cover the entire range of choice – from ptarmigan to capercaillie and from hare to fallow deer – but here are a few suggestions. If you've never tried them, why not bear them in mind next time you're looking for something different? The dates in brackets are the open seasons decreed by law for England, Scotland and Wales. In Northern Ireland and the Irish Republic there are a number of variations. As long as they were taken during the season, game birds and animals may also be sold frozen outside these dates.

Pheasant

(1 October–1 February) Easy to cook; good value (one plump bird should feed four); hen more tender and tastier than the cock – the much prized 'black' hen is best of all.

Partridge

(1 September–1 February) The young English variety (as opposed to French) is the connoisseurs' choice. More delicate flavour than

pheasant, but more expensive because you should allow one bird per person.

Mallard

(1 September–31 January) Succulent; lends itself to lovely recipes for sauces and glazes; one bird feeds two. Not particular what it eats so can occasionally be on the fishy side.

Teal

(1 September–31 January) Very small; one per person. Diving duck, so feeds exclusively on vegetation; excellent flavour; sought after.

Snipe

(12 August–31 January) Tiny wader, really only large enough to serve as starter; delicate flavour.

Hare

(Open season all year round, though by tradition should not be taken on Sundays or Christmas Day) Rich flavour; marvellous value – a good-sized hare will feed about four. Jugged hare is a British classic.

Rabbit

(No close season) Cheap and versatile (curry, pie, stew, etc.); tastes more robust than chicken.

Venison

(Open seasons vary according to species, sex and whether you're in England and Wales or Scotland) Best roasting joints are haunch or saddle (the more expensive of the two). Virtually no fat so very low in cholesterol; tender, especially when marinated in red wine with juniper berries. The roe deer has the best flavour, with finer-grained meat than the red deer.

The sika is also good eating (the Gurkhas ordered some when their Colonel-in-Chief, Prince Charles, came to supper). Venison is now farmed (though the wild variety is held to be superior) and rapidly growing in popularity. However, most of what we produce still goes for export.

If the birds you plan to cook are feathered your best bet is to ask a friendly butcher to pluck them; most will for a small charge.

If you need to hang them first, choose a space where there's a draught, such as a bicycle shed, or a garage, and hang them head uppermost, so the juices drain into the body cavity. When the tail feathers pull out easily, they're ready. This may take from two to seven days, depending very much on temperature and humidity.

It pays to buy game from a licensed game dealer, whose prices won't reflect the overheads and perfectly legitimate mark-up of the High Street retailer. Unfortunately, not all belong to the National Game Dealers' Association. The failsafe method of finding a licensed game dealer is to telephone your local council and ask for the Environmental Health Office or the Legal Office.

Venison is becoming more popular as news of its extra-lean properties gets about. The British Deer Farmers' Association is doing its best to satisfy demand for the different cuts. For a copy of *The Good Venison Guide*, listing suppliers across Britain, send a stamped, addressed envelope to:
British Deer Farmers' Association,
Fairfields House,
5 Rough Knowler Wood,
Westwood Heath,
Coventry CV4 8GX.

R E C I P E S
MICHAEL BARRY

GAME PIE
Serves 4

Cooking game frightens people and this recipe is a marvellous introduction to how easy it is. It's also a very good introduction for people who are reluctant to eat game if they haven't tried it before. The pie looks so appetising and is so cheering and comforting to eat that it easily wins over doubters. Use any kind of game for this pie because it's an ancient recipe designed to use up what was available. Venison, hare, wild rabbit, wild duck, pigeon, pheasant and even grouse or partridge can go into it. You need about 2½ lb (1.1 kg) and, if pushed, can use one kind of game, let's say a pigeon, and bulk out the rest with stewing steak. This was also a traditional English custom when times were a bit thin on the game front.

This is a hot game pie, not the kind you leave to get cold and serve in slices. It's meant to be eaten as the main course in autumn or winter. It's nicest to eat if you can find a moment to take the bones out of the meat, either before or after cooking. By the way, you can make your own puff pastry, of course, but I have suggested buying it – it's much craftier.

2½ lb (1.1 kg) assorted game, or game bulked with stewing steak
1 tablespoon olive or vegetable oil
1 onion, studded with cloves
2 bay leaves
1½ pints (900 ml) water
2 tablespoons cornflour
1 level tablespoon made mustard (grain, Dijon or English)
4 oz (100 g) baby onions (frozen are fine)
8 oz (225 g) button mushrooms
Salt and freshly ground black pepper
1 × 8 oz (225 g) packet of puff pastry, thawed if frozen
Beaten egg, to glaze

Cut the game into small pieces and remove the bones. (Alternatively, this can be done after the meat has been cooked but before the pastry is added.) Sauté the game in the oil until brown, then put in a deep pie dish with a flat rim. Add the onion, bay leaves and water, cover with foil and cook at 350°F (180°C), gas mark 4, for about 2 hours if using venison in the pie. Wild duck, pigeon and pheasant will cook more quickly – check them after about 1 hour.

When the meat is cooked, take the pie dish out of the oven and remove the onion and bay leaves. Mix the cornflour and mustard with a little water and stir into the cooked game stock. Add the baby onions and mushrooms and mix. Season with salt and pepper. Roll out the pastry. Rub the flat rim of the pie dish with a little water to moisten it and cover with the pastry, pressing it on to the wetted rim. (This will help it stick.) Trim off the surplus pastry and use to make leaf or flower decorations. Brush with a little beaten egg, make a cut in the centre and bake at 425°F (220°C), gas mark 7, for about 30 minutes, until the pastry is golden. Serve with mashed potato and red cabbage.

CHRISTMAS GOOSE
Serves 6

Though we now think that turkey is *the* Christmas bird, it's dominance is comparatively recent. For centuries geese were the top choice, and now they are making a late-twentieth-century comeback. This is partly because of our considerable appetite for nostalgia, but it is also a sure sign of our rediscovered interest in more complex and mature flavours. Though domestic goose isn't really game, the rich and strong savouriness is closer to that of wild game birds than to the blandness of our modern poultry.

This is not likely to be a dish to most children's tastes. Mine certainly prefer turkey, so save it for a Christmas lunch that's for adults only, or for a festive supper over the longer holiday that we seem to enjoy these days. Geese are now widely available both fresh and frozen. Choose one around 6–7 lb (2.7–3.2 kg) and expect it to feed six people only once.

Although when craftily cooked goose *isn't* greasy, it *is* rich. The sharp apple sauce goes especially well with it. So too does red cabbage cooked as on page 50, and mashed or new potatoes.

6–7lb (2.7–3.2 kg) goose, thawed if frozen, at room temperature
4 Spanish onions, chopped
1 egg
1 tablespoon sage
2 oz (50 g) fresh breadcrumbs (*not* artificially coloured ones!)
Salt and freshly ground black pepper
1 lb (450 g) Bramley apples, peeled, cored and chopped
1 oz (25 g) butter
Pinch of ground cloves
2 oz (50 g) sugar

Wash the goose carefully and then place it in a clean sink. Pour a kettle of boiling water over it, turning it half way. Let it drain and then dry for 2 hours. This will help give a crisp skin and prevent greasiness.

To make the stuffing, which is not essential but nice, mix the onions with the egg, sage and breadcrumbs. Season generously, then stuff the cavity. As with all stuffings, don't pack it in too tightly. Put the bird on a rack over a roasting pan and roast at 375°F (190°C), gas mark 5, for 20 minutes per 1 lb (450 g), plus 20 minutes more. Take the goose out of the oven and leave it to stand for 15 minutes in a warm place. Use the fat for other things if you want but don't be tempted to try to turn it into gravy. Instead use this sharp spicy and very traditional sauce. Gently cook the apples with 1 tablespoon water until soft. Add the butter, cloves and sugar, then simmer 15 minutes, until well blended; you can make it sweeter but try it with the goose first.

To carve the goose, remember it's easier and safer to carve the breast into three sections a side than attempt delicate slices. The drumsticks, thighs and wings, much smaller than on a turkey, make up the rest of the portions. Don't forget to serve the stuffing – it will have taken on a delicious flavour.

OFFAL

One of the faults of modern butchers (and there are several) is that they don't stock offal very often, if at all. Unfortunately carcasses are usually delivered to them with these delicious bits already removed for the mysterious purposes of the food manufacturing industry. We should all demand offal from our butchers – and here are some suggestions as to what we could do with it when we get it home.

In the north of Italy there's a famous dish made from shin of veal called ossobucco. Shin of veal is virtually impossible to obtain in this country so I've adapted the delicious Milanese way of cooking shin to our own oxtail – a very delicious and nutritious cut that deserves far better than the ubiquitous soup. In other countries it's treated very differently. There's a French recipe that involves cooking it with grapes, and a splendid Indian curry, but this particular recipe has as its special charm the garnish traditionally added in Italy, made of freshly chopped garlic, lemon rind and parsley. It's called a *gremolata* and, even if you're not a garlic lover, you'll find that the combination of flavours and piquancy this adds to the long-simmered stew is really worth trying. Yellow rice is the traditional accompaniment, but you could try mashed potatoes, or even pasta.

OXTAIL CASSEROLE
Serves 4

The majority of good butchers and supermarkets should sell oxtail. At less than £1 per 1 lb (450 g) it's good value. For this recipe, ask the shop to slice the oxtail through the bone into slices approximately 1 inch (2.5 cm) thick.

2 lb (900 g) oxtail, cut into 1-inch (2.5-cm) slices
2 tablespoons olive oil
8 oz (225 g) onions, chopped
1 clove garlic, crushed
18 oz (500 g) thick tomato purée, or 18 oz (500 g) tinned chopped tomatoes
½ teaspoon each dried oregano, thyme and basil
Salt and freshly ground black pepper

For the garnish
2 cloves garlic, finely chopped
Finely grated rind of 1 lemon (organic)
2 tablespoons chopped fresh parsley

Fry the oxtail pieces in olive oil until browned. Add the onions, garlic, tomato purée, herbs and seasoning. Cover and simmer for 4 hours, either on top of the stove or, preferably, in the oven at 300°F (150°C), gas mark 2. You will need to check at regular intervals to ensure it stays moist; if the casserole starts to dry out, add a little water. At the end of the cooking time, mix the garnish ingredients, place the oxtail on an oval serving dish and sprinkle with the garnish, or serve on a bed of long-grain rice coloured with saffron.

CRISPY TRIPE
Serves 4

Now before you give up in disgust, I used to hate tripe too. Then I discovered this way of cooking it. It's an adaptation of a number of different techniques I found in Mexico and in southern France round Lyon. The method may seem long-winded but most of the time the tripe's cooking itself, so it's a fairly effortless as well as economical dish. The first time I serve this to people they usually think it's a more exotic, but equally delicious, dish of calamari cooked in breadcrumbs. Do try it. It benefits from a sharp tartare sauce or even a chilli-flavoured tomato sauce as it might get in South America. It makes surprisingly good finger food for a buffet, too, if well drained before serving.

1 lb (450 g) prepared tripe
Salt
Squeeze of lemon juice
1–2 eggs, beaten
Fresh white breadcrumbs (made from 3 or 4 slices with crusts removed)
Vegetable oil for deep-frying

Poach the tripe in salted water containing a squeeze of lemon juice for 1 hour. Drain and set aside to cool, then cut into chip-size pieces. Coat in the eggs and breadcrumbs. Deep-fry for about 5 minutes, until crisp and golden. Fry in batches if necessary. Drain on paper towels and serve with a dipping sauce. Yoghurt with French mustard and a pinch of garlic salt is very nice for this, or tartare sauce.

LIVER IN PIQUANT SAUCE
Serves 4

One of the reasons liver gets such a bad culinary press is that it is often overcooked. With some liver, ox liver in particular, a lengthy cooking is essential because it's quite tough, but with calf's or lamb's liver, 1 minute is enough for a ½-inch- (1-cm)-thick slice. You have to serve it very quickly because, cooked as briefly as it is, it barely gets hot right the way through and, therefore, cools down very rapidly as well.

A good sharp sauce sets liver off nicely and the one I suggest here is derived from a very easy American way of making gravy for hamburgers and other steaks when they've been pan-fried in salt. Don't worry about the salt here, just dip the liver in the seasoned flour and have everything else ready to go as soon as it's cooked. It's 2 minutes from start of play to the first bite, so get family or friends seated first.

1 lb (450 g) calf's liver, thinly sliced (lamb's liver will do)
Plain flour seasoned with ground bay leaves, paprika and salt
1 dessertspoon vegetable oil
2 teaspoons Worcestershire sauce
1 tablespoon lemon juice
1 dessertspoon butter
Pinch of finely chopped fresh herbs, such as parsley, sage or thyme,
or a mixture

Coat the liver in seasoned flour. Heat the oil in a frying pan and briskly fry the liver slices for 35–40 seconds on each side. Transfer to a serving dish and keep warm. Add the Worcestershire sauce, lemon juice, butter and herbs to the pan. Stir over a high heat for 30 seconds to amalgamate, then pour over the liver and serve immediately.

PAMPAS-STYLE OX HEART
Serves 4

Down in the pampas, the great South American grasslands of Argentina and Uruguay, where the corned beef comes from, they have a special way with the bits that don't go into the tins. They're particularly fond of ox heart. Not surprising really when you consider that once it's trimmed it's very low in fat and rich in flavour. So much so that some unscrupulous restaurateurs have been known to cut ox heart into very thin slices and serve it as duck. But back where the gauchos ride, they have a slightly different way of dealing with it, and each region has its own speciality. This one is simple and makes a warming casserole or stew for chilly nights. The ground cummin can be bought in any Indian or ethnic shop, sometimes called *jeera*.

1 lb (450 g) ox heart, trimmed and cut into 1-inch (2.5-cm) cubes
2 tablespoons vegetable oil
8 oz (225 g) green or red peppers, cored, seeded and sliced
8 oz (225 g) onions, sliced
½ teaspoon ground cummin
½ teaspoon chilli powder
8 oz (225 g) thick Italian tomato purée or tinned tomatoes
Salt and freshly ground black pepper

Fry the ox heart cubes in the oil to brown. Transfer to a flameproof casserole with a slotted spoon. Add the peppers and onions to the pan the heart was cooked in and sprinkle in the spices. Stir over moderate heat for 1–2 minutes. Transfer to the meat, together with the purée or tomatoes and season. Cover and cook at 325°F (170°C), gas mark 3, for 1½ hours. Serve with boiled rice or baked sweet potatoes.

KIDNEYS IN MUSTARD SAUCE
Serves 4

Kidneys are traditionally a 'man's dish' for some reason. In the gentleman's clubs around Pall Mall in London, these used to be served at breakfast time, though I think the dictates of healthier eating have elbowed it back to lunch, or even dinner these days. This is a very light way of cooking kidneys which many people, even those slightly doubtful, find themselves eating with enjoyment. In the clubs it's served with little crisp triangles of bread fried in butter and with duchesse potatoes (mashed potatoes that have been beaten with egg and piped into fanciful shapes, then baked for 10–15 minutes). They are well worth making, especially if you've got some mashed potatoes left over from another meal, because they don't have to be eaten immediately they're made but can be piped and left until you're ready to cook. The fried bread can be very usefully replaced with triangles of wholemeal toast, adding a little crunch to go with the richness of the sauce.

1 lb (450 g) calf's or lamb's kidneys, trimmed
1 tablespoon vegetable oil
1 tablespoon butter
1 small onion, finely chopped
8 oz (225 g) button mushrooms, halved if large
1 tablespoon French mustard (Dijon or Bordeaux)
4 tablespoons double cream
Salt and freshly ground black pepper

Slice the calf's kidneys in ½-inch- (1-cm)-wide pieces or halve the lambs' kidneys. Sauté in the oil and butter, to brown lightly, then add the onion and cook very gently for 10 minutes. Add the mushrooms and turn in the juices for 3 minutes. Transfer the kidneys, onion and mushrooms to a serving dish with a slotted spoon. Pour the mustard and cream into the pan and stir while bringing to the boil. Pour over the kidneys and season generously. Serve at once with fried bread or wholemeal toast.

GRATIN OF SWEETBREADS
Serves 2 as a main course, 4 as a starter
Although Britain has a great tradition of eating offal of all kinds in previous periods of our culinary history, sweetbreads have rarely enjoyed any kind of success. This is a great pity because, of all offal, they are the most delicate, easily digested and least capable of giving offence. In other countries they are used in a wide variety of ways: sometimes their creamy smoothness is used to enhance pâtés or terrines, and at other times they are pressed, breadcrumbed and fried to make very crispy little cutlets, or threaded on to skewers to make exotic kebabs. Sweetbreads are widely available these days in supermarkets, especially lamb sweetbreads, which are imported in quite significant quantities from New Zealand.

Prepared in small quantities and baked in tiny gratin or ramekin dishes, this makes a very rich and filling first course for a grand dinner party. As a main dish, I think nothing goes with it quite so well as freshly cooked leaf spinach, lightly buttered and generously peppered.

1 lb (450 g) sweetbreads
Salt
1 tablespoon lemon juice
2 oz (50 g) Cheddar or Gruyère cheese, grated

For the sauce
½ pint (300 ml) milk
1½ tablespoons plain flour
1 tablespoon butter
Pinch of English mustard

Wash the sweetbreads carefully and soak in cold water for 10 minutes. Drain and poach the sweetbreads in plenty of salted water with the lemon juice for about 10 minutes, until tender. Drain and set aside to cool, then trim and cut into walnut-sized pieces. Make up a thick white sauce using the milk, flour, butter and mustard (see page 48). Mix the sweetbreads into the sauce and pour into a gratin dish. Sprinkle with the cheese and bake in the top of a hot oven, 375°F (190°C), gas mark 5, for about 15 minutes, until it's brown and bubbling. Serve immediately.

D R I N K S
JILL GOOLDEN

MATCHING WINES WITH FOOD
Quite a few people have a view on which wine to serve with fish or red meat. But what goes best with a rich flavour like game? Or with vegetarian dishes? Or with poultry? Well, it all depends on the strength of the dish...

Now that most of the cobwebs that used to surround the so-called etiquette of wine have at last been swept away, we can all see much more clearly what is what – thank goodness! – and there really is no need to worry about being caught out doing the wrong thing.

Wine, like beer or Coca-Cola, is made to be drunk and enjoyed, not agonised over. So the new chorus is that (virtually) anything goes. You should drink what you like, when you like and how you like, exploring and experimenting as you go along. And that applies to choosing wines to go with food as well – either a casual supper, or when entertaining more formally – but only up to a point...

To enjoy your cooking and your favourite wines to the full, ideally they ought to complement each other in some way. You wouldn't serve a hot lime pickle with poached fish because it would quite simply blast it off the plate, overshadowing its delicacy and subtlety. In the same way, a powerfully spiced kebab would kill a slight white wine stone dead, and a hefty heavyweight red wine would completely swamp an innocent sweet.

So the key is, where possible, to match weight with weight, to keep an even footing on the dryness/sweetness scale, to partner together similar strengths of flavour. These are the simple guidelines.

Matching weight with weight is a relatively simple business: the lighter dishes (usually white meat or fish) team well with light white wines, and the heavier recipes (red meat, rich sauces) are best suited to heavier reds. Chicken represents the middle ground, and can take either a red or a white wine – it's simply a matter of personal preference which you go for – although you might be influenced by the way the meat will be cooked: chicken in a creamy white sauce might favour white wine; roast chicken, red, white or even rosé, and coq au vin, definitely red.

Partnering similar sweetnesses together is, again, quite a logical marriage to make. Too sweet a wine with, say, roast beef would dominate and detract from the satisfying simplicity of the joint. Savoury and sweet tastes don't usually blend together well on an equal basis – one has to be very obviously in the minority for the partnership to work and, ideally, the food and wine should have more or less equal status on the dining table. Some medium-sweet white wines will marry well with fish dishes but, as a rule, it is safer to keep the sweeter wines until last to accompany the pudding or dessert, and to lead with your drier wines. In terms of strength of flavour, a dish such as poached fish would be classified as low, roast chicken as low-to-medium, steak and kidney as higher, and venison as highest. If you know your way around, wines can be as straightforward, but if not, there are a few pointers – shown in the information box – which will help.

The strength-of-flavour guide to wines

Lower strength flavour
Most dry white wines, especially those made in Europe. Typical examples: Muscadets, most French vins de pays, rosés from the Loire.

Low to medium flavour
White wines from California, Australia, Germany, white Riojas from Spain.

Medium strength
'Spicy' grape varietal wines such as Muscat and Gewürztraminer, the Olasz and Laski Rieslings from Eastern Europe. Plus lighter, fruitier red wines such as Beaujolais, Lambrusco, Valpolicella.

Higher strength flavour
Most are red, such as wines from Bordeaux and Burgundy. Most less expensive reds fall into this category too.

Top whack
'Big' reds from Australia and the Châteauneuf-du-Papes from the Rhône in France, both including the same grape variety. Also the older Riojas and the Californian Zinfandels.

APPLES, PEARS & OTHER DESSERTS

INTRODUCTION
CHRIS KELLY

After a disappointing visit to his greengrocers, Chris set out to discover what has happened to the Great British Apple.

Whatever would have been the effect on the Christian account of Genesis if the Serpent had offered Eve a Golden Delicious in the Garden of Eden? Like any discerning fruit-eater, she would almost certainly have said: 'Look, it's very kind of you, but quite frankly, I find them rather boring. I suppose you wouldn't by any chance have a Laxton's Epicure, would you? Or a St Edmund's Pippin?' Since the temptation presumably took place several million years before the discovery of either of those lovely varieties (or, indeed, of the apple itself – but let's not complicate matters unduly), the Serpent's answering hiss might well have been decidedly unbiblical. And we'd all be strolling around without benefit of fig leaves; always assuming, of course, that we were strolling around at all.

If the domestic apple had an Eden, it was Britain; although we can't claim that it first took root here. The fruit is thought to have had its origins in Trans-Caucasia (the region we now call Armenia and Georgia), ideally placed at a crossroads of trade routes and population migration. We know the Romans cultivated apples and we suppose that they brought some varieties with them to these chilly islands in the wild west of their empire. The climate may have come as a nasty shock to legionaries raised on the balmy shores of the Mediterranean, but for the apple it turned out to be perfect.

Long after the Romans decamped, much of their enthusiasm for horticulture found disciples in the monasteries. Our most famous fruit and vegetable market grew out of the sale of surpluses from the convent garden in London, with its great meadow known as the Long Acre. The earliest named native English dessert apple was the Pearmain, in the thirteenth century, and a pioneer among cookers was the Costard (hence 'costermonger', or so they say).

Thereafter, the development of apple varieties in Britain went hand-in-hand with the cultivation of gardens by the nobility, eager both to form collections and to provide delicious choice for themselves and their guests. By the reign of Henry VIII, fruit farming had begun on a modest scale. The King sent his fruiterer to France, which was light years ahead in food appreciation and culinary skills. The envoy came back with Pippins, which he planted in Kent, from where they spread throughout the country. Despite the efforts of aristocratic enthusiasts, however, most of the fruit sold in London was still imported (though what state it was in when it arrived, four and a half centuries before the advent of chilling, is hard to imagine).

For its Golden Age, the British apple had to await the indefatigable Victorians. The greatest public collections boasted over 1000 varieties, and many a country house orchard grew 100 or so; some specifically for cider-making.

So, what went wrong? Why is it that less than a century after the heyday of the British apple, I walk into my local supermarket in the spring and find just four varieties of dessert apple on the shelves – three of them kindly provided by France, South Africa and Chile, and only one therefore – the ubiquitous Cox – representing the home side. I know April isn't exactly prime time in our native orchards but even when the season is more favourable, the selection will not reflect a fraction of our rich heritage.

The answer lies in the dreaded word 'rationalisation'. After the Second World War, when fruit growing began to pick up again, commercial suppliers looked for the most profitable options. French orchards re-stocked with an American variety – the Golden Delicious – a regular-shaped, heavy cropper which looked good in the box and was relatively easy to store. Faced with this formidable competition when Britain joined the EEC, we put our money on an apple which, though very tasty at its best, has certain undeniable drawbacks. The aforementioned Cox does not crop as heavily as the Golden Delicious, it is susceptible to disease, it is more difficult to grow well and store, and it is not uniform in shape. In 1986, this slightly problematical fruit accounted for 63% of our dessert apple production. (In the same year, 87% of the culinary apples commercially produced in Britain were Bramleys.)

Scientists have prolonged the Cox's season (the apple is naturally at its peak in November) by putting it into suspended animation in controlled-atmosphere stores, but one unfortunate result has been a marked loss of flavour. Quality has also suffered as a consequence of early picking.

Fortunately, all is not yet lost. The National Fruit Trials at Faversham are constantly looking for viable commercial alternatives to the Golden Delicious and the Cox. A leading contender is the Jonagold, raised in the United States and available from November/December through to spring. Crisp and rosy-cheeked, with a good balanced flavour, it has also impressed growers because it's a good cropper and keeps well (although Jill's view of the Jonagold is a little less sanguine . . . see page 114). Another apple winning professional supporters is the Gala, an offspring of Kidd's Orange Red, which began life in New Zealand. Like the Jonagold, it's pretty, crisp, juicy, flavoursome and winters successfully even in amateur conditions.

Perhaps our best hope of a re-emergence of choice, however, lies with individuals who care passionately enough about the British apple to fight for its survival: enthusiasts like Dr Joan Morgan. Brought up on a farm in the Vale of Glamorgan, where every smallholding had its orchard, she was shocked on moving to London to find the range of British apples on sale diminished year by year. Trained as a research bio-chemist, Joan made it her business to find out everything she could about our native cookers and eaters. The Royal Horticultural Society gave her the run of their fruit collection at Wisley, where she tried and/or cooked every one of the more than 600 varieties. Joan now spends much of her time spreading the word about our one national treasure that actually does grow on trees.

A neighbour of Joan's in Kent, pomologist Peter Dodd, is a staunch ally in the great crusade. A lecturer in horticulture at Wye College, Peter is in demand overseas as a consultant/adviser.

Closer to home, Peter feels strongly that the British consumer has been low on the list of fruit growers' priorities. He stresses, however, that if we demand greater choice, then the commercial producers will have no option but to comply. We've seen the effect of public pressure on the brewing industry; there's no reason why we shouldn't register an equally spectacular triumph in the orchard. In all fairness, though, we must be prepared to settle for fruit which is not perfectly shaped, and we must recognise that it will be more expensive to compensate for lower yields. We may also have to subdue our understandable (even laudable) distaste for chemical sprays. Without these, Peter says, it would be impossible to produce apples commercially. For all that, it's still a sobering thought that commercial apple crops are sprayed more than 20 times a year with fungicides and pesticides.

As to the commercial prospects for British pears, Peter is less than optimistic. Despite the fact our most successful variety, the Conference, does relatively well on this side of the Channel, he still describes it as a 'turnip' compared with the Comice grown in France and Italy. The climate here remains marginal, he says, and we can't consistently grow top quality fruit.

Meanwhile, pending that happy day when our supermarket shelves are brimming with a colourful, crisp and cheery array of British apples, we must either beat a path to farm shops, or grow the fruit ourselves. If you choose to do the latter, here's a short list of recommendations from Peter Dodd – remember that you'll generally need to grow more than one variety to ensure regular cropping: Discovery, Katy, Jonagold, Gala, Ribston Pippin, Rosemary Russet, Golden Noble (cooker).

If you want to plant your own apple trees and you have a medium-sized garden, ask for M9 root-stock; if it's tiny, try M27. *The Observer Good Gardening Guide* has a useful summary of many suitable varieties for amateurs to grow and offers advice on how to do it. The most comprehensive reference work is Harry Baker's *The Fruit Garden Displayed*, published by the Royal Horticultural Society, the paperback edition of which can be found in good booksellers at £6.95. Alternatively, you can write (enclosing a self-addressed envelope and a cheque or postal order for £8.05 made payable to The Royal Horticultural Society) to:
The Information Centre,
Royal Horticultural Society,
Wisley,
Woking,
Surrey GU23 6QD.

For the less ambitious apple-fan, the choice available in farm shops will obviously vary according to geography and time of year. Here are some round-the-calendar suggestions from Joan, with no guarantees that they'll necessarily be available where you live. If they are, however, she says you'll be delighted with them:

AUGUST/EARLY SEPTEMBER

Discovery Round, bright red, with cream flesh sometimes stained pink.
Miller's Seedling Kentish apple, cream flushed with pink and red stripes; flesh crisp and glistening with juice.

SEPTEMBER/OCTOBER

St Edmund's Pippin (aka *St Edmund's Russet*) The connoisseur's choice. Golden, almost completely covered in russet; flesh dense and richly flavoured, with a hint of pear; must be well ripened.
Ellison's Orange Hardy; especially popular in the North of England; greenish yellow with an orange-red cheek; flesh perfumed, sweet, with well balanced acidity, developing slight aniseed flavour.

NOVEMBER/CHRISTMAS

Blenheim Orange Addictive, but hard to find. Yellow, with a red cheek and some russeting; flesh pale cream, sweet, crumbling, with flavour of nuts. Larger ones are great for apple Charlotte.
Egremont Russet Golden, developing orange cheek under the light brown russet; flesh dense and distinctly flavoured; early in season, fruity, nutty taste.

DECEMBER/FEBRUARY

Orleans Reinette Yellow, with red cheek covered in fine network of russeting; flesh cream, sweet, with intense nutty flavour; aromatic.
Ashmead's Kernel Green/yellow, with red/brown flush; stripes and fine russeting; flesh white, firm, juicy, sweet, with plenty of acidity.

LATE APPLE THAT KEEPS WELL

Kidd's Orange Red Conical-shaped, with scarlet flush; sweet, with some acidity; intense, delicate, flower-like taste. Needs plenty of sun and should not be picked too early.

If you feel like a change of cooking apple from the splendid Bramley, and you're lucky enough to find one of the following varieties, try:

AUGUST/SEPTEMBER

Early Victoria Good for baked apple or apple sauce.

OCTOBER, KEEPING UNTIL CHRISTMAS

Golden Noble Big, golden, sharp and fruity.

NOVEMBER, KEEPING UNTIL MARCH

Wellington Old-fashioned classic; probably available in West Midlands. Cooks to creamy, juicy, sharp purée.

OCTOBER, KEEPING UNTIL MARCH

Howgate Wonder Very large, conical; dark crimson flush and stripes on a green background; sweet sub-acid flavour; mild by comparison with Bramley. Also stays firmer in cooking than Bramley.

RECIPES
MICHAEL BARRY

Although apples and pears are our most common fruit, they are often taken for granted. Like Chris, I think this is a great pity because they can make some of the most delicious puddings and savouries. Here are four recipes with some very different origins. Most go back a long way into culinary history – the pear tart, for instance, is very French in style because it was in the early nineteenth century that the French growers began developing the pears we now enjoy. But first, a recipe that's come back to Britain having already crossed the Atlantic once before in its lifetime.

AMERICAN APPLE PIE
Serves 4–6

There's a strong suspicion that many years ago, when the Pilgrim Fathers set up shop across the water, we made our apple pies over here in a very similar way to this. But then we changed the pattern and began to make shallower and shallower pies, often with pastry just on the top. This recipe goes back to that older tradition and has the American addition of cornflour, which means that the slices are thick and succulent, not floppy and runny.

8 oz (225 g) shortcrust pastry, thawed if frozen
1 lb (450 g) Bramley apples, peeled, cored and sliced
1 tablespoon lemon juice
1 tablespoon cornflour
3 oz (75 g) caster sugar
1 teaspoon each ground cinnamon and ground cloves
1 egg, beaten, to glaze
Extra caster sugar (optional)

Thinly roll out half the pastry on a lightly floured surface to about ¼ inch (0.5 cm) thick. Line a greased 1½-pint (900-ml) pie dish with half the pastry. Put the apples into a bowl, add the lemon juice, cornflour, sugar and spices and gently mix together. Pile into the pastry case, making a mound in the centre to keep the pastry lid from sinking. Cover with the remaining pastry, pressing the edges to seal. Make two incisions in the centre for the steam to escape. Trim the edges and glaze with the beaten egg. (The trimmings can be used to make decorations.) Sprinkle a little caster sugar on the top to give a crunchy texture to the pastry, if desired. Bake in a preheated oven at 350°F (180°C), gas mark 4, for 35–45 minutes until golden.

APPLE CLAFOUTIS

Serves 4–6

A clafoutis is a giant fruit pancake and really needs to be eaten hot to be appreciated. It owes its high reputation in the annals of French gastronomy to the brief period when the huge bitter-sweet black cherries are in season in south-west France. If you can get the great big sweet black cherries that come from Kent for about two or three weeks in the year, do make it with those. But it's also traditionally made with apples. In France they use an apple called Reinette but in Britain most of our cooking apples also make a very good version. My favourite is mentioned by Chris in his introduction – the Howgate Wonder. It's a cross between a Blenheim Orange and other apples and has a flavour and scent that's unique. Cream, though it's not traditional in France, is, I think, a smashing addition. So, too, is one of the richer plain yoghurts, such as the Greek varieties.

5 eggs
5 oz (150 g) plain flour
5 oz (150 g) icing sugar
1 tablespoon vegetable oil
1 lb (450 g) cooking apples, unpeeled, cored and diced
4 oz (100 g) mixed dried fruit, such as raisins, sultanas and ready-to-eat
dried apricots
2 tablespoons caster sugar
1 teaspoon ground allspice (optional)

Beat the eggs, flour and icing sugar together, or blend in a food processor, until the mixture resembles a batter. Add the oil and mix the batter again. Pour the mixture into a greased oval or round gratin dish, making sure the dish is deep enough for the fruit. The mixture will rise, so use a dish at least 1½ inches (4 cm) deep. Combine the apples, dried fruit and caster sugar and distribute evenly over the top. If using allspice, sprinkle it on top of this mixture. Cook in a pre-heated oven at 375°F (190°C), gas mark 5, for 30–40 minutes. Serve hot.

PEAR AND ALMOND TART

Serves 8

This is a French-style tart with a double filling, one of almond frangipani and one of poached pears. You can use tinned pears at a pinch, but it's much better to peel, halve, core and poach your own for about 10 minutes in a syrup made from 4 oz (100 g) sugar and ½ pint (300 ml) water. The tart is very spectacular and should be served with a whole pear half in the centre of each slice. It's delicious warm and scrumptious cold.

1 quantity Pâte Sablée (see below)
2 oz (50 g) butter
2 oz (50 g) caster sugar
2 oz (50 g) ground almonds
1 oz (25 g) self-raising flour
½ teaspoon almond essence
1 egg
4 pears, or 8 pear halves, poached (see above) and cooled

Thinly roll out the pastry on a lightly floured surface. Use to line a 10-inch (25-cm) flan ring. Cream the butter and sugar together for the frangipani. Add the remaining ingredients except the pears and knead together. Fill the pastry case with the mixture. Place the poached pear halves on top like spokes on a wheel, pointed ends to the middle, then bake at 425°F (220°C), gas mark 7, for 25–30 minutes, until the pastry is crisp and the pears are tender.

PÂTE SABLÉE

This is the ultimate French sweet pastry – literally 'sandy pastry', because when you eat it it crumbles under the tongue. You can make it by hand or use a food processor.

8 oz (225 g) plain flour
2 tablespoons caster sugar
4 oz (100 g) butter, well chilled
Pinch of salt
1 egg

If you're using a processor, put all the ingredients, except the egg, in together. Then add the egg and – gradually – enough water for the dough to form a coherent ball around the blade of the processor.

By hand, work the flour, caster sugar and butter together with the salt until the mixture resembles fine breadcrumbs. Work in the egg and about half an eggshell of water, until the pastry clings firmly together.

Knead briefly, roll it into a ball and allow it to rest in the fridge for 30 minutes before using.

HOME-SWEETENED YOGHURTS

These two recipes are simple and super-quick ways of flavouring plain yoghurt. Both are infinitely adaptable; you can substitute ingredients, change quantities and add your own touches to make your own individual tastes and textures. Apart from this flexibility, one of the great benefits of making flavoured yoghurts this way is that you know what's in them – you can control the amount of sugar that goes in. The first, with honey and walnuts, is based on flavours I always associate with Turkey, where thick, golden yoghurt made from sheep's milk, wonderful dark thyme-scented honey and fresh walnuts combine to make the most wonderful breakfast. Good supermarket yoghurt, a little runny honey and some nuts of your own make a passably satisfactory substitute.

HONEY AND WALNUT YOGHURT

Serves 4

3 tablespoons runny honey
18 oz (500 g) natural yoghurt
3 tablespoons crushed walnuts

Warm the honey until it's fairly liquid, then stir into the yoghurt. If the yoghurt is one of the pre-set kinds, beat it until it's a little liquid itself before adding the honey, or they won't mix satisfactorily. Mix in 2 tablespoons of the walnuts, then pour into pretty stemmed glasses and decorate with the remaining walnuts.

QUICK FRUIT YOGHURT

Serves 4

This crafty recipe relies on good jam. There is now a wide range of very good-quality low-sugar jams – they're often referred to as 'high fruit' as well. They're made in a large number of different places and the important thing about them is that the flavour, texture and sweetness all come from the fruit itself and not from additives or unnecessarily large quantities of sugar. Home-made jam is, of course, ideal and the flavour you use depends on your own predilection. For a really unusual kind, though, if you haven't got any home-made greengage, go and buy some and try it – it's absolutely one of my favourites.

18 oz (500 g) natural yoghurt
3 tablespoons good-quality low-sugar jam

If the jam is very stiff, melt it a little over low heat before beating into the yoghurt. Pour into an attractive bowl and serve with crispy ginger biscuits.

We asked a group of student nurses to taste a range of yoghurts to see which they liked best. There's a considerable spread of varieties on the market, with most supermarkets supplying their own brands. The new Greek-style yoghurts are widely available, as are both whole and skimmed milk yoghurts, set and runny. Of the normal yoghurts, the tasting team liked the Greek-style ones best, because of their creamy smooth texture, and their lack of bitterness. The Greek-style yoghurts are 'drained' yoghurts, so they have a higher fat content than most plain yoghurts. However, they are much lower in fat than single cream. They therefore make an ideal alternative in any cooking in which they won't be boiled. If you boil a sauce with yoghurt in, there's a fair chance that it will separate unless you've stabilised the sauce before cooking with a dessertspoonful of cornflour.

Of the specifically low-fat yoghurts, St Ivel 'Shape' was the favourite amongst the testers.

MAKING YOUR OWN YOGHURT

If you're making yoghurt, be careful what you use as a starter, because some varieties, particularly imports from Greece, have been pasteurised to improve their keeping qualities. This means they are 'dead' and there are no live bacteria in them to act as a starter for your batch.

Boil 1 pint (600 ml) milk, with 2 tablespoons skimmed milk powder stirred in, for 5 minutes. Allow to cool to blood heat (cool enough to put your little finger in for 10 seconds without screaming). Stir in a generous tablespoon of *live*, natural yoghurt (it must not be pasteurised). Place in a covered bowl in a warm place for 6 hours and you'll have your own fresh yoghurt. An insulated flask is ideal for this process, if you've got a wide-necked one.

SUSSEX POND PUDDING
Serves 6
This is a traditional recipe from the South-east of England. There are two versions, one from Sussex and one from Kent. The only

difference seems to me to be that the Kent one includes dried fruit, particularly currants, whereas the Sussex one doesn't. Either way, they're an unusual twist on the old concept of suet pudding.

While the pastry is suet, the flavour which predominates is the scent and bitter-sweetness of the lemon, an unexpected centrepiece. In the light of the new information about fungicide waxes, you may wish to get an organic lemon, or one that hasn't been waxed, to make this pudding.

8 oz (225 g) self-raising flour
1 egg
6 oz (175 g) vegetarian suet (a new idea – widely available – which helps cut down the animal fat)
About 5 fl oz (150 ml) water, to bind

For the filling
4 oz (100 g) butter, diced
4 oz (100 g) soft brown sugar
4 oz (100 g) currants (for the Kent version)
1 lemon (unwaxed if possible)

For the custard
½ pint (300 ml) milk
1½ tablespoons caster sugar
1 teaspoon vanilla essence
½ oz (15 g) cornflour
1 egg, beaten

Make the pastry with the flour, egg and suet, by hand or in a blender or food processor, adding just enough water to make a soft malleable dough. Roll out on a lightly floured board to ¼ inch (0.5 cm) thick. Using two-thirds of the pastry, line a 2-pint (1.1-litre) pudding basin, keeping the rest for a lid. Fill the basin with half the butter, brown sugar and currants, if using. Then, using a sharp, thin instrument (a hat pin is ideal), pierce the lemon all over and stand in the pudding on the filling mixture. Top with the remaining filling ingredients so the lemon is covered. Cover with the pastry lid and seal firmly round the edges.

Cover the basin in buttered foil, pleated to allow for steam expansion during cooking. Tie up with enough string to leave a handle on top for easy removal, then steam for 3 hours in a saucepan, or 1 hour in a pressure cooker.

While the pudding is steaming, make the custard. Mix the milk, sugar and vanilla together and heat thoroughly until the sugar is dissolved. Add the cornflour, creamed with a little of the milk, and whisk until smooth. Add the egg to the custard. Heat gently, whisk and keep hot. Try not to boil it too much. Remove the pudding by putting a serving bowl over the basin and turning both upside down. Make a cut in the suet pastry so that the juice flows out, forming a 'pond'. Serve with the custard.

CHRISTMAS 'PUDS'

For our Christmas programme we had a quiz. I and Michael Smith, the food writer and television chef (who almost single-handedly with the help of *Upstairs, Downstairs* and *The Duchess of Duke Street* resurrected traditional English cooking), had to create a pudding suitable for Christmas Day in 2 minutes. Michael's was a model of self-indulgence, guaranteed to bring on instant Christmas-itis, but looked and tasted wonderful. Mine, on the other hand, rather more simple, was more beneficial to those parts that the traditional Christmas pudding reaches only too easily.

FRUIT MALAKOFF by MICHAEL SMITH
Serves 4–6

This is really a kind of Christmas pudding ice and needs to be made at least a day in advance to give it plenty of time to set. It can be presented very simply, or dressed up very grandly. It's so rich, you'll only need to serve a small quantity to each person.

4 oz (100 g) butter
4 oz (100 g) icing sugar
4 egg yolks
4 tablespoons dark rum
4 oz (100 g) mixed glacé fruit, such as cherries, pineapple, apricots
4 oz (100 g) walnuts, finely chopped
4 oz (100 g) hazelnuts, finely chopped
Boudoir biscuits or meringues, to decorate

Cream the butter, sugar and egg yolks together. Mix in the rum, fruit and nuts. Spoon into a 1½ pint- (900-ml)-mould and chill until set, preferably overnight. Turn out on to a dish and decorate the sides with boudoir biscuits or meringues made from the egg whites.

HOT PINEAPPLE FRUIT COCKTAIL
Serves 4

You can serve this recipe in an ordinary pudding bowl if you like, but my method turns the shell of the pineapple into an exotic serving dish in its own right. The technique sounds difficult but is really simplicity itself. You draw a noughts and crosses board on each cut half of a pineapple, making sure the knife doesn't go through the outer shell but gets close to it. A good strong spoon will then prise the cubes out without any effort.

Don't cook the fruit too long or it starts to turn into jam. You have to eat it hot because it congeals quite rapidly, but eaten at the right moment it is one of the great puddings of the world.

1 pineapple, halved lengthways, with leaves left on
2 oz (50 g) butter
4 oz (100 g) preserved ginger in syrup, chopped
2 satsumas, peeled and segmented
2 tablespoons soft brown sugar

Scoop out the flesh from each half of the pineapple by scoring with a sharp knife, first downwards and then across, then scoop the squares out with a sharp spoon. Melt the butter in a frying pan and add the pineapple. Heat through with the ginger, satsumas and brown sugar for 1½ minutes. Pour the mixture back into the pineapple shells and serve immediately.

FRUIT JUICES

JILL GOOLDEN

Some apple juices are delicious, others mediocre... how can you pick the better ones? Most orange juices are dull ... how can you make your own? Jill has the answers.

APPLE JUICE

Twenty years ago apples were hardly being juiced. The massive healthy eating and drinking boom that has swept us all so fitly into the seventies and eighties had yet to gather momentum. Many of the luscious fruits of the English apple orchards had still to be tapped.

We were an impoverished race as a result. Anyone who allowed the deliciousness of freshly pressed apple juice to pass them by has seriously been missing something very good. For real *fresh* apple juice (which can, by the way, very easily be obtained in grocery shops, health food shops and supermarkets) is one of the decade's great treats.

I don't want you to think I'm some sort of a crank warbling on like this about a simple drink out of a carton. But I have only recently seen – or, should I say, tasted – the light, and fully admit to all the ardour and fervour of the new convert.

Over the years, I have certainly clocked up more tasting practice with wines (and to a lesser extent spirits) than any other drinks. It hadn't occurred to me that a straightforward tasting of fruit juices – or, even more precisely, apple juices – could be anything like as interesting and diverse. But I had a revelation in store.

Apple juices can *easily* be as different one from the next as wines. The range of appearances alone is remarkable: some are dark golden and clear, while others are cloudy and pale. Then there are the dark conker-coloured juices, opaque and 'thick'. The range of scents is extensive, too. Before I met my Damascus at the *Food and Drink* apple juice tasting, I had never registered that apples have such a delicious pungence.

And that's to say nothing of the actual *taste*. The range of flavours – and, as importantly, *qualities* – among apple juices is infinite. And often not strictly related to price. There are bargains to be had. Delicious, fully-flavoured apple juices smelling and tasting as fresh as an apple off a tree compete with much weedier, less convincing specimens.

There is an enormously wide discrepancy in taste, texture and even pungence between the different varieties of apples. Even if, at worst, your greengrocer or supermarket limits the choice to either the imported Golden Delicious or the ubiquitous Granny Smith, you'll appreciate the huge differences that can exist. The Golden Delicious is a 'woolly' fruit, and although crisp on the outside, it is not very dense – in fact, not really much of a mouthful at all – and it has little scent and not a very concentrated flavour.

Granny Smiths, on the other hand, are crisp all the way through, with tough skins and tightly packed flesh. They do have a highly identifiable, individual smell and a bitter-sweet taste, the skin being rather tart, and the pulp fresh and sugary. So, when you consider it, there is little in common between the two. And that's only two different apple types from a possible cast of thousands. Now you should see that the range can be much wider than you had perhaps thought.

The type, or range, of apples used in a blend has, of course, a vital bearing on the end result. But it is not the only factor affecting the taste and quality of apple juice. There is the method used to extract the juices, and the two are closely linked . . . I don't want you to skip on to another chapter now, imagining that I am going to become all technical and bore you to pieces with my new passion for apple juice. I'm not, I assure you – I have some very practical recommendations to make.

But it has to be said that the production method is one of the really important parts of the story. The easiest way to tell the quality of the juice you're going to buy is from the outside of the carton. Essentially there are two very different methods for getting juice from apple to glass; and the method has a strong bearing on the end result.

The great majority of apple juices are not made simply by squeezing the juice out of a batch of apples and transferring it into bottles. Instead, once the juice has been obtained and clarified, it goes into an 'evaporator', where, subjected to great heat under a vacuum, it is reduced to a sticky mess. For every 9 litres (16 pints) apple juice going into the evaporator, only 1 litre (1¾ pints) sticky syrup comes out.

Curiously, the aroma is taken off and concentrated in a separate operation where 150 litres (264 pints) are needed to produce just 1 litre (1¾ pints) of aroma. This (presumably intensely smelly) cache of apple scent is then used to add aroma back into the reconstituted concentrate when it is eventually made up into juice.

The main purpose of making apple juice concentrate is so that cheaply grown apples from far and wide (Hungary, for instance, is a favourite spot) can be used to make juice anywhere . . . at any time. Sometimes this method is adopted as a rather elaborate storing technique. All juices made in this way must be clearly identified on the bottle or carton as 'Made from concentrated apple juice'. You can avoid them if you want.

Alternatively, you can look for 'fresh pressed' apple juice, which finds its way, virtually unadulterated, from tree to bottle or carton, then to glass. This is simply the pressed juice of apples – English ones if the label says so.

Conveniently, when considering apple juices you really can afford to be patriotic. Where apples are concerned, we genuinely excel. You might have fondly imagined that virtually all apple juices are English. They certainly appear to be from the label. But there is a twist. The majority are made in Britain from concentrated apple juice imported *from abroad.* The water used to reconstitute the apple concentrate back to a normal-strength juice is British, I'll grant you that, but not the apple ingredient itself.

As Chris pointed out earlier, our British climate is the very best for growing apples. There are few fruit that actually benefit from having too much sun, and apples, in particular, respond very well to the often unkind conditions. Everything in the orchard calendar happens slowly, and through a long-drawn-out growing season, with only spasmodic sun, the fruit develops gradually, packing in as much concentration of flavour as possible. The traditional English types of apples that are part of our national heritage are those best suited to our ideal climate.

Apples grown abroad don't enjoy the natural advantages of the British *pommes*. Too much sun makes them race through their conception, infancy, childhood and adolescence, growing up altogether too quickly for their own good. They make full-size fruit in double quick time, puffing up like a cotton wool ball. There is no time for the flavour to catch, let alone to concentrate, and the natural aromas don't really have a chance to get a grip. All in all, the Continental apple is generally a pretty wishy-washy specimen.

Certainly such fruits as the Golden and Red Delicious, and their near relation the Jonagold (grown prolifically on the Continent, and often used to make juice concentrate), are a very good commercial bet for the farmers who raise them, because they grow in great abundance and very rapidly. But they are not the ideal for the customer – neither, in my view, to eat, nor as a foundation for the 'concentrated' form of apple juice.

Take the evidence of the blind tasting I referred to earlier. Lined up in opaque cups, so you could see neither the appearance nor the identity of each juice, a full array of apple juices was placed in front of me and apple expert Dr Joan Morgan so we could sort out which we liked best. There were 40 varieties to try and, as it turned out, a vast discrepancy between the ones we liked least and those we enjoyed most.

Extraordinarily, as we discovered when the bottles and cartons were unveiled, neither of us gave a single 'concentrated' version a mark as high as any of the 'fresh pressed' juices. They seemed dull, rather 'artificial' and often over-sweet, bearing little or no resemblance to real apples when you analysed the scent and taste.

Looking back at my tasting notes, I see I described the concentrated apple juices as: 'chemically', 'burnt', 'dead', 'pear-like', 'syrupy', 'sickly', 'soapy', 'watery'. The fresh pressed juices were in a completely different league. They were all delicious, in one way or another, and provoked such remarks as 'intense blossomy fragrance', 'fruits and flowers', 'complex', 'strong taste of Cox's', 'powerful apple scent', 'mouthfilling', 'genuine', 'magnificent', 'mouth-watering' . . . I warned you I got a bit carried away!

So a juice made from concentrated apple juice is liable to fail on two scores: on the inferior nature of the fruit from which it is made, and on the procedure it must go through during its production. My advice is to look at the carton and avoid the concentrates.

The best juices are made from freshly pressed English apples, and say so loud and clear on the label. These are made quite simply from good-quality, ripe apples, which are milled and crushed. Vitamin C (ascorbic acid) is generally added as an anti-oxidant and the juice is pasteurised to keep it stable. And the whole process from apple to bottle or carton takes only a couple of hours.

Cox's are a favourite variety for fresh pressed juices, along with Bramleys, contributing the necessary zest of acidity, plus numerous other splendid English apples. Many of the fresh pressed apple juices are blends of different varieties (in the same way as many wines are in fact blends of different types of grapes), all chosen to complement each other to give a harmonious whole. Often the label will declare which varieties have been used.

A few producers make 'single variety' juices, which I found the most astonishing of all when tasted 'blind'. I had heard apple experts could tell one variety from another simply from the juice. I wasn't sure I could even tell one variety of *apple* from another, but it was more obvious than I thought. The individuality of the single varieties shone out of the cup and on a couple of the more obvious I could pick them out quite easily from an array of 40 or more. Worcester stood out in an intensely individual way and Bramley was pretty easy to spot on its own too, being so unforgivingly tart.

Apple juices made from a single variety of apple are, unfortunately, a rarity. You find them most easily in apple-growing and cider-making districts, either in local health food shops, or at the farm gate. Many are pasteurised, such as the excellent Duskin range, available in quaint old glass jars in the Canterbury area. Duskins do Discovery, Bramley, Cox, James Grieve and Worcester, available all year round. Farms without the necessary equipment for pasteurising can still make apple juice, but it must instantly be deep frozen, and only sold in the frozen state.

Single-variety apple juices available nationally are even more of a rarity. Copella bring out a kind of Beaujolais nouveau of an apple juice early in the apple season, made from one of the earliest varieties, the Discovery, available for only a short period. Revells of Ross-on-Wye pride themselves on their clear Golden Russet, made from the concentratedly sweet, almost nutty, Egremont Russet, available year round.

Bramley used to be the longest lasting apple which, if kept in cold storage under a blanket of gas to exclude all the oxygen, would remain usable for up to 12 months. Now a long lasting dessert apple has been identified as well, the Crispin. So fresh apple juice can continue to be made year round from fresh apples. Copella and Aspall are the two largest producers of freshly pressed English apple juice, providing many of the supermarkets with their 'own label' juices. Both also make some more exotic freshly pressed juice mixtures. Particularly delicious, in a thoroughly unsweet, adult way, are Copella's apple and strawberry and morello cherry and apple. Aspall's apple and blackberry is lovely and autumnal, too.

A curious kind of protocol has evolved in the packaging of apple juices, between the bottle, the 'tetrabrik' type of oblong carton, and the more elegant gable-top carton. The bottle came first, and so has a place as the most regal of containers. It scores points for keeping juice in good nick, and can keep it in good nick longest. It is, of course, the most expensive form of packaging. The squat little tetrabrik is customarily used for 'long life' juice; filled to the seams with no room for air at all, it can keep the juice in good condition for about six months. And here is the anomaly. The elegant gable top, slim and tall, has evolved as the classic 'up market' container for fresh juice. It is the status symbol among apple juices, suggesting only a 10-day life until the sell-by date. Gable tops jostle together in chill cabinets, the cartons having been cosseted and chilled since they were first filled. You possibly pay an extra 10p–15p for that extra cosseting.

But the juice in all probability started out just as the long life juice did. All commercial apple juice is pasteurised, but because the 'smarter' gable top leaves space at the top for the intrusion of air, the apple juice underneath can – and will – go off much faster, needing plenty of Tender Loving Care. Because we associate this gable-top carton with the top of the range, some juices made from concentrate rather than freshly pressed fruit use it as a disguise to try to pass themselves off as the Real Macoy. So beware! Read the small print carefully.

You can make your own apple juice at home but it's really only for the fresh juice fanatics. The equipment is expensive, quite bulky

---

Apple juices particularly recommended from Jill's blind tasting

Safeway's Fresh English Apple Juice
Copella's Farm Pressed English Apple Juice
Aspall's Apple Juice
Waitrose's English Natural Apple Juice for a rather sharper taste (lots of Bramleys included – good for cooking with, incidentally)

Not only are these juices scrumptious to drink on their own – they are also delicious poured over muesli for breakfast. Or, more wickedly, instead of tonic, with gin.

---

and very difficult to wash up. To cap it all, you have to drink home-made apple juice right away because it quickly oxidises and turns a dirty brown. Most of the commercial juices I have mentioned have Vitamin C added to keep them an acceptable colour.

But if you are interested in making juice at home, don't give up hope. Read on...

ORANGE JUICE

When it comes to orange juice, like it or not, you have little alterna-tive to buying reconstituted concentrated juice. That's what all carton orange juice is. And, I'm sorry to say, that's what it tastes like as well, suffering all the same drawbacks as the apple concen-trates.

I know it's very popular and drunk a lot but, to my tastebuds, it bears little resemblance to the original fruit. Some of the supermar-kets sell freshly pressed orange juice made on the premises from oranges, and it emerges full of convincing 'bits', lusciously fresh and with that marvellously refreshing bite of acidity. You can take it home, to be consumed within three days, or so they say. Don't be-lieve a word of it! It actually starts to go off in hours, and tastes really rather unpleasant (even worse than the carton stuff) long before the 'use-by' date. What's the solution?

Maybe to 'squeeze your own', and drink it right away. To find out the best ways of making your own citrus juice, we asked home economist Daphne Metland to look into the alternatives, and she discovered that if you buy oranges at their cheapest (we bought them for 32p per lb (450 g) for the survey) you can squeeze your own juice more economically than you can buy the ready squeezed juice, and you don't need *that* elaborate or expensive a gadget to

Results of the *Food and Drink* 'squeeze-your-own' test

The Magimix food processor or Kenwood mixer with citrus juicer attachments (both attachments around £10) emerged with credit. *Cost of juice:* £1.40 per litre (1¾ pints), excluding the price of the equipment.

Ordinary lemon squeezers do a good job. Best recommend-ation was the jug juicer from David Mellor for £5.67, with different-sized gauges for oranges or grapefruit. *Cost of juice:* £1.59 per litre (1¾ pints).

Top of the small electric juicers: the Braun at £10.95. It was quick, effortless and easy to clean. *Cost of juice:* £1.59 per litre (1¾ pints).

do a good job. But some of the gadgets we've listed are time-consuming to wash up, so you'll need to add that to the price you pay for a fresh flavour.

While testing the various machines at home, Daphne Metland enlisted the support of her family to taste the results. The tasting panel duly assembled (her two young children) and delivered its verdict. Neither of its members liked the freshly squeezed juice very much. 'It's full of bits' was the reaction from her seven-year-old, while a screwed-up face from her three-year-old revealed that it seemed rather tart to a young palate. Daphne regrets that she had previously given them the standard orange juice made from concentrate – the experience had clearly led them to expect clear, very sweet juice.

However the type of orange you buy can make a great deal of difference – some varieties are much sweeter than others. Also, thin-skinned oranges contain more juice. It's worth picking them up in the shop, feeling the weight (the heavier the better), and looking for raised ends which denote a lot of pith and less juice.

One final note – experiment with different citrus mixtures. Orange and grapefruit is delicious, and blood oranges make a pinky-red drink that's only for the stouthearted and followers of Count Dracula.

COMMONWEALTH COOKING

INTRODUCTION
MICHAEL BARRY

The British Empire, lest we forget, was very much a two-way street. At its height, and the Commonwealth reflects this, it stretched from southern China to South America, and from Arctic Canada to almost Antarctic New Zealand. The influence this extraordinary confederation has had on our food is not only still with us, but growing by the day – whether it's mango chutney from India, lamb from New Zealand, or lime juice cordial from the West Indies.

Today there is an even more direct influence on the way that we eat. The large numbers of Britons from Commonwealth countries who live here provide a whole range of both 'eating out' and 'eating in' opportunities we've been very quick to take advantage of. There are few small towns in the most rural parts of Britain these days that don't boast a Chinese or an Indian take-away. There's a Cypriot doner kebab shop round many a corner and the ethnic markets and food stores that have sprung up offer a culinary adventure with spices and exotic ingredients alongside the more familiar tins and packets.

A visit to a street market in South London can give you a flavour of just how exotic our taste and opportunities have become. Take Hillbrook Street in Balham, 15 or 20 years ago an ordinary British weekend street market, but on a Saturday morning nowadays a walk along the stalls is a real geography lesson. Starting at one end, a Polish émigré runs a marvellous fruit stall in the old traditional style. Next to him there's a wet fish stall with exotic tropical species lying amidst the herrings and whiting. Then, a West Indian fruit stall, specialising in mangoes and limes, green bananas as well as ripe ones, plantains and pumpkins, recognisable vegetables and some that, unless like me you've had the good fortune to live in the West Indies, look rather strange. Then there is a stall selling ordinary English salad vegetables, but behind it a fishmongers where shark and flying fish, pomfret and octopus nestle amongst and sell as well as cod, salmon and haddock. So it goes up the street. Stalls specialising in yams and sweet potatoes, alongside one selling local farm fresh brown eggs. The four butchers in the street are English, Mauritian, Pakistani and Kenyan, and some of the grocers are as expert in varieties of Nigerian palm oil as others are in organic yoghurt and English cheeses. It's a very exciting place to shop and I always go home laden with far more than I meant to buy.

It's not just in street markets that you find this variety. In supermarkets from the east coast of Kent to the west coast of Wales, I've found vegetables and bean sprouts ready for stir-frying, Indian curry pastes and condiments, spices, Chinese noodles, mangoes and mangosteens, papayas and poppadoms. Not in specialist shops but in ordinary supermarkets with native-born British people buying and enjoying them. Whatever the political or economic outcome of the Empire and the Commonwealth, culinarily we must have sown well, because the harvest we are reaping is rich and delicious.

I've a great taste for what used to be thought of as Commonwealth food, but now must be seen as *new* British food. Time spent living abroad (including the West Indies and Africa), and a large Indian family in half my ancestry, has left me with a taste for the three main strands of the new British cooking – Indian, West Indian and that from Hong Kong, which means Cantonese. This is the southernmost part of China with a famous and distinctive cuisine of its own, based very much on shellfish and seafood. It has a lightness and sweet sharpness that we've come to regard as 'sweet and sour'.

We have become used to the idea of Chinese food as all being cut up very small to be eaten easily with chopsticks. In fact, although it is always eaten with chopsticks, Chinese food doesn't always come in little stir-fry pieces. The recipe I've given here is for a whole fish, deep-fried in the Cantonese manner and served with a very special sweet and sour sauce. If you don't have a fryer big enough for the whole fish, cut it up or even cook it in fillets the same way. The important thing is not to cut it up into tiny pieces because then the effect of crisp outside and succulent inside is lost. I've suggested a stir-fry vegetable dish with some exotic as well as some well-known ingredients. The whole meal is best eaten Chinese-style with cooked rice, techniques for which you will find below.

Chinese techniques with rice

The Chinese don't use the long-grain rice usually used in Indian food, but a medium grain that has a little stickiness to it so that it can be easily picked up with chopsticks when it's cooked. Any medium-grain rice, but not pudding rice, will cook very well in this way.

Measure the rice into a cup or container by volume. You need about 2 oz (50 g) per person, so a ½-pint (300-ml) mug will contain about the right amount for four people. Put it into a saucepan with a good tight-fitting lid and measure twice the volume of water, using the same mug. Pour on to the rice, then add a good pinch of salt and a couple of drops of cooking oil. Stir together, bring to the boil and turn the heat down to the absolute minimum. Cover the pan carefully with a folded tea towel, which will absorb the steam and avoid the rice getting too soggy. Be sure to keep the tea towel well away from the heat source. Put the lid on and leave to simmer for about 20 minutes. When the rice is cooked it will have absorbed all the water and have little vent-holes on the surface. You can keep it warm by turning the heat off and leaving the lid on for up to another 15 minutes or so without any harm.

To serve, break it up a bit with a fork, helping the grains to separate a little, but leave enough residual stickiness to make them perfect for eating with chopsticks.

RECIPES
MICHAEL BARRY

HONG KONG
SWEET-AND-SOUR FISH
Serves 4

2 lb (900 g) round fish, such as sea bass, whiting, grey or red mullet
2 tablespoons cornflour
Vegetable oil
1 carrot, very thinly sliced
1 tablespoon soy sauce (light or dark)
1 tablespoon brown sugar
1 tablespoon cider vinegar
4 tablespoons chopped pineapple chunks, or crushed pineapple
3 spring onions, cut into thin slivers, to garnish

Wipe the fish and, if it is too long to go into your deep-fat fryer in one piece, cut it in half across the middle. Rub all over with some of the cornflour and deep-fry for 5 minutes. In a small pan, fry the carrot in 1 tablespoon oil for 1 minute. Add all the other ingredients except the onions, and stir over a gentle heat until thick and shiny. Lay the fish out in its original shape, dress with the sauce down its length and garnish with the onions, concealing the cut if you made one.

EXOTIC STIR-FRY
Serves 4
Have all the ingredients prepared before you start to cook. Be sure to cut the peppers to the same size as the water chestnuts or bamboo shoots so they cook in the same amount of time.

1 tablespoon vegetable oil
1 teaspoon finely chopped fresh root ginger
1 clove garlic, crushed
8 oz (225 g) bamboo shoots, or water chestnuts, thinly sliced
1 red pepper, cored, seeded and chopped
1 green pepper, cored, seeded and chopped
Pinch of salt
1 dessertspoon soy sauce (light or dark)

Pour the oil into a hot heavy-based wok or frying pan. When the oil is hot, add the ginger and garlic and stir-fry for 1 minute. Add all the bamboo shoots and peppers to the pan and stir, gently and continuously, for 1–1½ minutes. Add the salt and soy sauce and continue stirring for another minute. Serve while the vegetables still have a crisp bite to them.

NORTH INDIA

Like China, India has an enormously varied cuisine with different regions having different culinary traditions – some vegetarian, some meat-based, some using lots of dairy products and others none, some very mild and some very highly spiced. The meal I'm suggesting here is one of my absolute favourites. It's quite mild and very rich. It comes from the north of India, around the region of Delhi and the valleys that run up to the north-west frontier and Afghanistan. In the north of India, rice, although often eaten, is not the staple food. Wheat is more commonly eaten in a variety of ways and usually as a form of bread. The parathas I've suggested are typical of these breads, being made with a wholemeal flour and cooked very quickly and easily on a griddle. If you don't have a griddle, substitute a good thick, solid frying pan and don't worry if the first piece of bread doesn't work perfectly. It's my experience that you soon become expert enough to be turning them off at the rate of one a minute. Even Chris Kelly managed that – and on television, too!

If you think, by the way, this food is very mild, much Indian food is actually like this. I've had meal after meal across the subcontinent where chilli has hardly put in an appearance and it's a mistake to assume that unless the top of your head's coming off you haven't really eaten Indian.

LAMB TIKKA
Serves 4

5 oz (150 g) natural yoghurt
1 onion, sliced
1 clove garlic, crushed
1 teaspoon turmeric
1 teaspoon ground coriander
1 teaspoon ground ginger
1 teaspoon salt
½ teaspoon chilli powder
1 tablespoon lemon juice
1 lb (450 g) boned lamb, cut into 1-inch (2.5-cm) cubes

Mix all the ingredients, except the lamb, together in a bowl. You can replace the turmeric, coriander, ginger, salt and chilli powder with 2 tablespoons 'tandoori mix' powder if this is more convenient. Marinate the lamb in the mixture for at least 4, and preferably 12, hours.

Thread the lamb on to 4 skewers. Place these on a rack under a high grill that has been pre-heated for 15 minutes, or on a rack in a pre-heated oven at 425°F (220°C), gas mark 7. Cook, turning once, until browned all over – 5 minutes per side under the grill; 12 minutes in the oven.

NOTE: reserve the marinade if you want to make the potato recipe opposite.

PARATHA
Makes 4

3 oz (75 g) clarified butter
(or the concentrated butter now on sale)
10 oz (275 g) wholemeal flour
½ teaspoon salt
6 tablespoons water

Rub 2 oz (50 g) of the butter into the flour until it resembles breadcrumbs. Add the salt and water and knead to a smooth dough: this can be done in a food processor. Divide into 4 equal portions and roll out to the size of a small dinner plate. Dot the remaining butter over the parathas, fold each into quarters and roll out again. Heat a solid cast-iron pan and dry-fry each paratha in turn until brown; this takes about 1 minute. Turn and fry for another minute. Stack and keep warm until needed.

RAITA
Serves 4

½ teaspoon salt
1 tablespoon lemon juice
1 × 5 oz (150 g) carton natural yoghurt
4-inch (10-cm) piece cucumber, thinly sliced
2 tomatoes, chopped
½ green pepper, cored, seeded and thinly sliced
Handful of fresh mint leaves, chopped

Beat the salt, lemon juice and yoghurt together. Not more than 30 minutes before you're due to eat, stir in the cucumber, tomatoes, green pepper and mint. Add other salad vegetables as well if you like; spring onions and even cooked new potatoes – very thinly sliced – are quite common in India.

SPICY POTATOES
Serves 2–4
If you would like another vegetable dish to go with the meat, breads and salad, try this one. It's very simple and can be made with left-over cooked potatoes.

1 tablespoon ghee (Indian clarified butter), or unsalted butter
8 oz (225 g) firm boiled potatoes
2 tablespoons of the marinade from Lamb Tikka (see page 123)
½ teaspoon sugar
1 tablespoon lemon juice
2 spring onions, thinly sliced

Gently melt the ghee or butter in a small pan, then add the potatoes and the marinade. Gently heat through until the marinade has coated the potatoes and the liquid has evaporated. Stir in the sugar and lemon juice, toss the potatoes gently and add the spring onions. Warm through for 1 minute, then serve.

JAMAICA

West Indian food is an extraordinary mixture. The combination of French, Spanish, African and British influences has given the most robust, and yet often quite sophisticated, flavours and textures to a range of tropical ingredients that are now very widely available in Britain.

When I lived in the West Indies it was a great pleasure to go to the local market and see what was available every Saturday morning. There was locally caught fish, a variety of tropical fruits and sometimes the unexpected, like goat meat (to be made into the island's favourite curry), or lobsters and oysters (to be grilled over charcoal).

But whatever was available at market, the favourite Sunday lunch in Jamaica was always the same – Chicken Fricassée and 'Rice and Peas'. The peas, of course, are not really what we would think of as peas, but red kidney beans – known throughout the Caribbean as 'red peas'. The dish made from them is so popular that, in Jamaica, it's known as the 'coat of arms', meaning it's the island's insignia. The recipes given here might not be eaten as a normal sit-down meal, but possibly in a buffet on Sunday at lunchtime, surrounded by a number of other dishes: an avocado salad with a dressing made from oil and lime juice, fried plantain, and perhaps sweet potatoes (which are available all over Britain nowadays) baked like an ordinary potato for about an hour and eaten with butter, salt and lots of black pepper. The whole meal would probably be preceded by one of the soups for which Jamaica is so justifiably famous, and which have wonderful names such as 'strongback' (a rich fish tea) or 'cocksoup' (chicken soup made with dumplings and flavoured with thyme and spring onion). The recipes here, I hope, will give you a flavour and a taste for those exotic Sundays half way across the world. They are from Jamaica but similar dishes, with regional modifications, are eaten all over the Caribbean.

CHICKEN FRICASSÉE
Serves 4

1 chicken, jointed
4 onions, sliced
Juice of ½ lemon (optional)
1 teaspoon brown sugar (optional)
2 tablespoons vegetable oil
4 large tomatoes, chopped
4 fl oz (100 ml) water
1 clove garlic, chopped

Pack the chicken pieces with half the sliced onions for at least 4 hours or overnight; you can marinate the chicken and onion by adding the lemon juice and brown sugar, if you wish. Discard the onions and fry the chicken in the oil until it browns. Add the remaining onions, tomatoes, water and garlic. Simmer for 40 minutes, adding a little more water if the dish threatens to dry out.

RICE AND PEAS
Serves 4

8 oz (225 g) dried red kidney beans ('peas'), soaked for at least 4 hours, or use tinned
8 oz (225 g) long-grain rice
2 oz (50 g) coconut cream (available in block form)
2 spring onions, chopped
1 teaspoon dried thyme
1 small red chilli pepper, sliced (optional)

Drain the beans. Boil in plenty of water for at least 10 minutes, then simmer for 1½ hours, until tender. If using tinned beans, drain well.

Measure the rice into a jug and add enough water – and the diluted juice from the tinned beans if you wish – so there is twice as much liquid as rice. Put into a saucepan, add the coconut cream, spring onions, thyme and chilli, if using, and the drained beans and simmer about 15 minutes or until all the water is absorbed. Stir occasionally during cooking to ensure that the dissolving coconut cream is well blended.

DRINKS
JILL GOOLDEN

REAL & NOT-SO-REAL BEERS

In her search for an accompaniment to Michael's spicy dishes Jill examines what goes into traditionally brewed beers, and highlights several thirst quenching alcohol-free or low-alcohol lagers.

Undoubtedly the best drink to serve with hot and spicy dishes is a thirst quencher – for my tastebuds, specifically lager, which cools the mouth, quells the thirst and is complementarily 'savoury'. But, that being said, there are undoubtedly lagers ... and lagers, with as wide a chasm dividing the best from the worst as you are likely to see among apparent equals.

At the nub of the quality dichotomy is the little matter of ingredients. Traditionally, beers have been made from only four vital constituents: malt, yeast, hops and water. Some still are, but these are lamentably few. In this country, all sorts of other curious constituents creep in as substitutes, notably other starch-rich cereals and vegetables such as rice and potatoes, instead of the traditional malted barley.

And because these substitutes fail precisely to replicate beer made only from the traditional four ingredients, all sorts of chemicals are required to redress the balance, and give you a convincing pint – if rather unsatisfactory in some respects. Unfortunately, the majority of British-made lagers are bastardised versions of the Real Thing. So much so, that a new British lager sticking to the old brewing traditions (Samuel Smith's, for the record) booms the word *natural* all over the label, proving that it is certainly an oddity.

In Germany a purity law was enforced from 1516 until last year, which forbade the inclusion of any ingredients other than the original four in German-made beer for the home market. There are loopholes, of course, and the law, having just been overruled by the EEC, is, in any case, beginning to lose its grip. But there are still a number of 'pure' German beers on sale here which, with Samuel Smith's praiseworthy new brew, honestly do knock spots off their rivals, many of which are more the product of a chemistry lab than a brewery. The ones that won particular praise in a blind tasting for the programme are Lowenbrau and Hacker Pschorr.

For teaming a non-alcoholic drink with hot or spicy cooking, I have no hesitation in again recommending lager – of the low- or no-alcohol variety this time, of course. Huge strides have been made in the technology for producing lager beers either low in alcohol (which means in practice less than 1%), or with an alcohol content of 0.05% or less, termed as 'alcohol free'. And considering the difficulties, some of the results are highly commendable.

Essentially there are two methods. Either the beers are fully fermented, and the alcohol is then removed by a secret process, or the fermentation process is halted almost as soon as it begins. And there are praiseworthy brews to be found in either category.

Barbican was the pioneer in this field, and began life as a rather disappointing wishy-washy apology for a drink. But it has been relaunched with 'more lager taste', as the label says, and I agree Sometimes. The alcohol removal technique seems to be a shade touch and go, with great disparity between the best and the worst in any given brand. Having first won me as a fan, Barbican then quickly blotted its copybook again with a series of 'off' bottles. Kaliber seems to have more consistency, and is an excellent non-alcoholic drink ... for people like myself, who like a drink.

Among the low-alcohol lagers Dansk, brewed by Carlsberg, won the most praise in our blind tasting, even being preferred (by some long way) to two normal-strength lagers, slipped in without the tasters knowing. Clausthaler and Sainsbury's own label (made by Clausthaler) are good, full-bodied, yeasty beers, which have every chance of standing up to Michael's ethnic recipes.

WHISKIES

MALT WHISKY
JILL GOOLDEN

SPIRIT OF A GREAT TRADITION

Blended whisky and malt whisky are very different drinks ... why?
What are the distinctive properties of malts, and how do they differ?
What are the names of the widely available ones? Jill went north of
the border to find out.

Worms might not be the most thrilling feature of a nature study of
Scotland, I grant you. But consider them in the context of the
country's *history*, and they become positively stimulating – I refer to
the brightly burnished, smoothly contoured copper 'worms' leading from the top of an illicit whisky still down into the expectant col-
lecting vessel below.

Whisky is without doubt the most valuable asset that Scotland
has. The spirit of this great tradition of the glens has remained un-
altered – in essence, at least – from the moment it first became a
brilliantly glinting 'worm in the heather'. It is alleged the Celts
learnt to distil a fermentation of malted grain into spirit 800 years
BC, and the production of this intoxicating potion continued in one
way or another ever since. It was outlawed endlessly along the way
by the Scottish Parliament, and after 1700 by the British Parliament.
This drove the domestic stills underground – or, to be more precise, under the heather.

To deceive the authorities, copper jam pans were used for boiling up the brew, kept innocently in the larder. The other essential

paraphernalia, including the vital copper worm, would be scattered or hidden about to avoid detection if the authorities called. Now production is on a massive scale (the jam pan would only have been able to yield about a bottle a week), but still follows almost the same techniques.

Today's malt whiskies still derive from a fermentation of malted barley, gently dried over a peat fire and distilled in a copper pot still. The collected liquor is nurtured in oak casks for a number of years before (and this is the best bit) it is drunk.

But only about 2% of all whisky made now follows this precise course to the end, because the great trade in whisky today is in 'the blend'. Virtually all of us think of the common kinds of blended whisky as traditional Scotch rather than the more elevated malts. But blended whisky would have been quite unheard of in the early days in the glen.

Early this century, by which time the distillation of Scotch had become quite above board, there was a great hoo-ha up in the freezing north. The fuss stemmed from a squabble in a grocer's shop about whether or not whisky – largely grain whisky, as it happens – coming from a 'continuous' or patent still rather than a pot still could be sold as real Scotch. A Royal Commission had to be called in to sort out the matter. After a great deal of evidence for and against, it was declared both types of whisky – malt from the pot and grain from the more economical patent still – could claim to be Scotch.

All the best known whisky brands therefore are subtle blends between essentially mass-produced grain whiskies and a collection of highly individual single malts. I use the word collection advisedly, because the business of gathering together the perfect combination of whiskies to make a perfect marriage is an art. And a highly respected art, at that. Behind every great blend is a great whisky blender or 'nose', who knows his whiskies like a porcelain collector knows his Meissen or Ming. And there's certainly a great deal to know.

There are about 100 malt distilleries dotted about all over Scotland, and although they all follow virtually the same manufacturing process, each produces an individual whisky in its own style. A great nose can detect the subtle differences one from another.

Precisely why malt whiskies should be so different from each other, although there are family similarities between neighbours, is claimed to be a mystery. Chemists furrow their brows, test their tubes, programme computers – and even smash each microscopic molecule – to try to diagnose precisely what lies behind the differences. So far they have failed. Admittedly there are some obvious variables between distilleries, but they don't reply to the riddle on their own.

The water, for instance, almost invariably comes from the individual distillery's own spring or burn. I never believed this entirely possible until a recent visit to the Highlands, where I saw for myself that heather, water and, for many months of the year, snow, roughly carve up the land equally. I suppose I can be persuaded that there is a subtle difference in taste between waters from all the innumerable different burns. But that in itself isn't enough.

The precise design of the still, too, can vary from one distillery to another. It is said that every idiosyncrasy – the real cranks say every accidental dent – alters the flavour of the resulting malt. Its production is treated with such reverence and the benign copper giants – the stills – are coaxed along with such an enormous amount of care, that you almost lose sight of what type of spirit is actually in the making.

There are the various methods of heating the still to boil the 'wash' and convert it to steam to be considered. The timing of each process can vary; the malted barley can be dried with more or less peat smoke; the oak used to make the casks for maturing the spirit can have enjoyed different pasts. The micro-climate can alter fractionally from one glen to another.

There are lots of aspects that vary in detail, but they still don't add up to there being essentially 100 or so *different* malts. For the amateur to be able to appreciate some of the peculiarities, he or she must concentrate on the broader, more obvious character traits shared by members of the several distinctive malt families.

There are the Lowland malts, the Islay (pronounced, as far as I can tell, 'Isler') malts, the Campbeltown malts (a dying – some would say dead – race, having lost most members) and the largest, the Highland malts, which include the distinctive Speyside branch of the family, with their own family characteristics.

Whiskies classified as Lowland malts largely come from the Glasgow and Edinburgh area, the most southerly member of the family being Bladnoch, down in Wigtown, and in style generally live up to their name, being quite low key, soft and unassertive. Islay malts made on the western isle of the same name have been graphically described as resembling a cross between tarry rope and the whiff of an operating theatre, with a wafting sense of the sea thrown in. . . But there are Islays and Islays, from the powerful, wild, island character of Laphroaig to the comparatively subdued Bruichladdich.

There were more than 30 distinctive west coast Campbeltown malts once made on the picturesque Mull of Kintyre. They became extinct in their original form, all but two ending up as casualties of the natural evolution of the industry, being unwelcome components in the all-important blend. Too 'aukward' for their own good. The two remaining Campbeltown malts have tried to adopt the Highland style.

Highland whiskies come from a far-ranging belt of the country, stretching from the Isle of Jura in the south-west, across to Dundee up to the top of the country, slipping in Skye and the Orkneys for good measure. Again their name gives the game away, since these are rugged customers, less smooth, rougher and tougher than those from the Lowland area; drinks you can get your teeth into. The 50 or so Highland malts concentrated in the popular Speyside area (around Elgin and the mouth of the Spey) have a concentratedly 'sweet' scent – almost like honey – with a hint of honey and glycerine in the flavour.

Each of the malt distilleries matures some of the precious product of its stills as a 'single malt', going under the name of the distillery, to find a way for itself in the world on its own. The rest is either sold to blenders, or exchanged for other malts, so the distillery can make up a blend of its own. The all-important blender will buy or acquire perhaps as many as 50 different whiskies to make up his blend. Having such an intimate knowledge of the exact smell and taste of each distillery's whisky, he assembles his blend on paper first, calculating how much of each component he will require to make up a precise, consistent whole. Then he takes to the laboratory, where he will sample, or more precisely nose, 100 whiskies in a single session.

Grain whisky is a critical part of any blended whisky. It is essentially a clean-tasting spirit, sharp and astringent, though mellowing as it matures. And by law, *all* whisky must mature in wooden casks in a warehouse for at least three years. Malts sold to be drunk singly are generally aged for considerably longer (15 or 20 years is not unusual), and the type of cask used has a considerable bearing on the final flavour.

So important is the maturing cask's job that the coopers in charge of keeping the oak casks up to scratch are being trained to spot a musty stave at a sniff, to reject an off-smelling cask at five paces. New coopers are to be picked not just on the strength of their wood-working abilities, but on their smelling prowess as well. Sherry butts (the oak casks in which matured sherry served its time) used to be two a penny in Britain. They were the accepted vessel in which sherry travelled to its export markets, and they would arrive here in their thousands, and, having discharged their Spanish contents, they would have had no further use, except to lend themselves to the all-important business of maturing whisky.

As the shipment of sherry in bottles became the accepted practice, this convenient source of oak barrels dried up. New casks could be made from new oak (generally from a number of French and Spanish forests, each imparting a different flavour) or broken-down bourbon casks would be imported from America. The rules for making bourbon stipulate that the essential oak barrels may be used only once.

Bourbon wood, however, isn't deemed good enough for some malts. The big boys at the Macallan distillery (producing an assertive – and very delicious – Highland malt) decided sherry butts were the thing. Not just any old sherry butts, but they actually went to the lengths of buying and planting test barrels in different Spanish *bodegas*, to be filled with different sherries; a fino here, an amontillado there, and then again a bit of dry oloroso. Now they supply *bodegas* with butts specifically for the purpose of being able to ship them back to Scotland for maturing their precious whiskies. And a remarkable, mellow – some would say distinctively peppery – whisky consistently results.

The celestial atmosphere that permeates the distilleries is drawn up short in only one place in these hallowed temples of malt. And that is at the portals of the extraordinary anachronism of the 'spirit safe'. With a lengthy history of illegal distilling, smuggling and, after the introduction of excise duty in 1644, tax evasion behind the industry, the people involved were deemed unfit to be trusted. The *uisge beatha* (water of life) issuing forth from the pot stills had to be locked up. Flowing from still to receiving receptacle behind glass in a locked safe, seen, but untouchable, unsniffable, and most important of all, undrinkable.

An exciseman was installed at each distillery: a wretched figure, detested and vilified, his sole purpose being to see that not a drop of whisky could be savoured without first being recorded by the Inland Revenue. He was there during every step of the process, the only man with the vital key to the safe, the warehouse, the spirit. To get the better of this mole was some stillmen's sole aim. And some did.

After filling 'new make' (the fresh run spirit) into casks, a certain residue remains in the hose, and one exciseman, returning to the spirit store room, or vat, unexpectedly, saw the workers lined up in a row on their backs, their open mouths being filled in turn from the hose. In another conveniently sited distillery, a filling hose destined for the empty casks in the store room was sidetracked instead through the castle-thick walls . . . into the adjacent pub.

Then there was the whisky-carrying train at Rothes station in Speyside, held up for just long enough for informed workers to lie underneath on their backs, and hope to strike gold as they plunged their silent drills up through the floor.

Pilfering was not the only illegal practice the excisemen had to contend with. Illicit distilling and smuggling still continued on an impressive scale, too. A Victorian commentator in the 1880s – 100 years after the establishment of the oldest distillery still in use today – wrote that smuggling

> was . . . the staple occupation of the inhabitants . . . they went to it with a spirit and energy which, had it but been shown in the cultivation of the soil or any other useful industry, the fruits of it would soon have been seen in the improvement of the country . . .

A blended whisky is normally made up with a selection of 20–25 malts, and 2 or 3 grain whiskies, all matured in oakwood for a minumum of 3 years.

Malt whisky, when bottled as a single malt, the produce of one distillery, is usually matured for 10–12 years, again in oakwood.
   There are 4 main types of single malt Scotch whisky, each with its own distinctive flavour: Highland malts, Lowland malts, Islay malts and Speyside malts. Here are some of the most widely available:

Highland malts
Blair Athol, Dalmore, Glenmorangie, Highland Park, Isle of Jura, Talisker, Tomatin, Tullibardine.

Lowland malts
Auchentoshan, Bladnoch, Deanston, Glenkinchie, Littlemill and Rosebank.

Islay malts
Ardbeg, Bowmore, Bruichladdich, Bunnahabhain, Lagavulin and Laphroaig.

Speyside malts
Balvenie, Dufftown, Glenfarclas, Glenfiddich, Glen Grant, Glenlivet, The Macallan and Tamnavulin.

There was genuine pride among the Scots in doing their own thing, regardless of the English law. Everyone was involved in some way, even if only on the receiving end. In the early eighteenth century, to the eight licensed distilleries, dutifully paying up to the British Government, there were possibly 400 or more undeclared concerns, who benefited only themselves. As Robert Burns, the most famous of all excisemen, pointed out, 'Freedom an' whisky gang tegither.' He didn't hold the post for long.

MAKING THE MOST OF WHISKY

Some people prefer to drink their whisky straight. Others wouldn't dream of having it without ice. There are also those who like their whisky with lemonade or cola – and some who are fussier about the brand of mixer than the type of whisky ... You may think it's just a matter of personal choice, but if you want to make the most of your glass of whisky, a master blender gives the following advice.

But first let's put the record straight on just what's what. A standard blend speaks for itself; a deluxe blend is a blend of whiskies, all of which are at least 12 years old, and this will be stated on the label; and a malt whisky can refer either to a top-of-the-range single malt, named after a particular distillery, or to a lesser 'vatted malt' which is a blend of several malts from different distilleries.

And now to the advice: matching the type of whisky to the time of day is important, according to the expert. In his opinion, a standard blend is best during the daytime, particularly before lunch. A deluxe blend, on the other hand, is a good early evening or pre-dinner drink. Finally, a malt whisky is best after a meal. You could drink it after lunch if you are free to relax all afternoon ... but since it is rather a heavy drink, it's really best after dinner.

Having dealt with *when* to drink whisky, our consultant turned to the knotty question of *how* to drink it. In his view, a standard blend is at its best when topped up with quite a bit of cold water. If you happen to be in Scotland, the ordinary tap water is fine. If, however, you find yourself in a hard water area, such as London, or in a city with a heavily chlorinated water supply, you would be better with a bland bottled water. Deluxe blends take less water, or can be enjoyed straight if you prefer. Malt whiskies, however, really do deserve to be savoured on their own. Indeed some people might say this is the *only* way to drink a malt whisky, although a little water can be added to lighten the drink if you wish to serve it during the day.

Finally, the question of how to keep whisky. The short answer is 'don't!'. Although spirits are much more stable than wines or fortified wines, once the bottle has been opened, they do start to deteriorate, and to lose their freshness. At the very most, an opened bottle should be consumed within 6–9 months.

MEALS ON
WHEELS

INTRODUCTION
CHRIS KELLY

Food and Drink *loves a challenge; fortunately for the programme, so do top chefs. Anton Mosimann started the whole thing by cooking Sunday lunch for a Sheffield family of seven on their £10 budget. Michael Quinn picked up the gauntlet and prepared meals in a hospital and at the Exeter home of two old-age pensioners. In the 1986/7 series, Raymond Blanc took John Wilcock with him to France to taste the marvellous food his mother cooks. London restaurateur and cookery writer Prue Leith was next to take up the challenge.*

The test we devised for Prue was no less daunting than her predecessors' tasks. We asked her to create five dishes for a British Rail InterCity buffet. BR catering has improved considerably, but we still wondered if the passengers would welcome a change of menu. We chose a service which was already the subject of an experiment. On the Brighton–Manchester line, which crosses London, British Rail have introduced Choice Express, 'a new style of buffet offering passengers service at their seats'. It's related to the 'Cuisine 2000' project, where food is prepared and partly cooked in 'shore based' kitchens and rapidly chilled, then loaded into special trolleys aboard the train before being finished in electric convection ovens. The system, 'arguably the biggest single step forward in the entire history of train catering' (BR's words), is designed to encourage reliability and 'wider and more interesting menus'.

Prue, who spent years on the British Rail board valiantly battling for quality, had no option but to go for dishes that were cheap and cheerful; her allowance for ingredients on each hot item was just 40p. These dishes would then sell at around £1.75. If the mark-up sounds excessive, bear in mind that BR has to carry much heavier non-food costs than a high street snack bar. Prue decided to offer Spicy Bean and Sausage Hot-Pot and Pasta Shells with Cheese and Mushrooms. Her cold choice consisted of Tuna Dip with Crudités and tortilla chips, delicious Brown Sugar Meringues and Apricot Jalousie. (You'll find the recipes for each at the end of this chapter.)

After exhaustive tests at home, Prue travelled to Gatwick, where, in a cavernous kitchen with the help of an experienced assistant, she made and packed a couple of dozen portions of each item. The food was blast-chilled overnight, before being sent to Brighton station for the next day's 10.15 to Manchester.

In spite of unfamiliar surroundings, the greatest problem at that point was economic: how to concoct savoury and sweet dishes for next to nothing and yet present them as something different and desirable.

The job of a British Rail steward may not look particularly tough from where you sit, and it sounds pretty idyllic too – travelling, meeting people – what could be better? The truth, however, is somewhat different. Prue hadn't been on the train many minutes before she began to feel sea-sick, and the queasiness persisted all the way north. Was this just a beginner's complaint, she wondered? Not on your life, said cheery professional steward Danny Messenger. Friends of his have been taking daily sickness pills for 40 years. As starts go, this one was not particularly comforting. Neither did what followed improve matters greatly. Despite Danny's frequent exhortations over the public address system, the majority of passengers were content to remain anchored, blissfully unaware of the difference an Apricot Jalousie might make to their lives. At least Prue could draw some satisfaction from the fact that, of the few who did beat a path to the buffet, most preferred her creations to British Rail's.

Prue Leith clearly does not know the meaning of defeat. Smiling through the nag of biliousness, and shrugging off the reluctance of the public, she decided to tackle the crisis head on. Taking a firm grip on the trolley, ably guided by Danny, she set off in pursuit of sales. In the length of the first carriage, she learned several important, and painful, lessons. To begin with, thoughtless railway engineers neglected to build every line on the flat; like the rolling English road, the permanent way has its ups and downs. Prue quickly found that when the train climbed, she was in danger of being crushed to death by the trolley. When the rolling stock went downhill, she had the sensation of being dragged for a walk by a bull mastiff. Any lateral motion, meanwhile, sent her crashing into the seats on either side, marking her with what should be known as 'British Rail restaurant scars'. These distractions, however, were as nothing beside the central difficulty of threading a four-wheel object with a mind of its own through a passage barely wide enough to accommodate it.

As in all the best stories, suffering had its rewards. The Tuna Dip with Crudités and tortilla chips went down well, especially with families. Overall, however, the response was a little disappointing. Watching the exercise, I could see a number of reasons why people were slow to lay out their money. It was obvious, for instance, that passengers were shy about eating in the presence of strangers. It's different on an aeroplane because there everyone's fed at the same time. The timing of the train, too, was crucial. Those who boarded during the first half of the journey had already eaten breakfast; those who joined us in the middle probably planned to have lunch at the other end; and those who came aboard in the final stretch might well have lunched first. Even if they still felt peckish, a hot-pot was, perhaps, too substantial. That's why the light dip was so successful. A further trade barrier was erected by those who had brought their own food. Nevertheless, it struck me that Prue's greatest handicap was possibly the most fundamental – namely, suspicion of the unfamiliar.

True to form, Prue was philosophical about the exercise. The few dozen dishes sold had been enjoyed and rated good value. She thinks British Rail is on to a good thing with Choice Express, which can afford to use fresh, additive-free ingredients since the life-expectancy of the dishes is very short; the food unsold on our journey, for instance, would be dumped the next day. For their part, BR were much taken with a couple of Prue's creations, and were thinking about including them in their menu.

Exhausted and bruised though she was by the time we reached Manchester Piccadilly, Prue could count herself lucky that she hadn't been a steward in the days of steam. Then, according to BR veteran Peter Murrin, 'If you felt sick you got a clout round the ear.' The mincer was the chef's best friend, because it disguised a multitude of leftovers, and the junior was expected to clean the Chief Steward's shoes. It's a telling thought, though, that in those days you could have bought *seven* breakfasts for the price of just one of Prue Leith's dishes.

RECIPES
PRUE LEITH

TUNA DIP WITH CRUDITÉS
Carrot
Celery
Red peppers
Spring onions
Cherry tomatoes
Tortilla chips, to serve

For the dip
Equal amounts of cream cheese, mayonnaise and drained tuna fish

Wash the vegetables, then cut them into small, equal-sized sticks to serve with the tortilla chips. The dip is made by mixing together the cream cheese, mayonnaise and tuna fish.

PASTA SHELLS WITH CHEESE AND MUSHROOMS
Serves 4
4 oz (100 g) mature cheese, such as Cheddar, grated
15 fl oz (450 ml) White Sauce (p. 48)
½ oz (15 g) butter
6 oz (175 g) open mushrooms, sliced and fried in butter
1 clove garlic, crushed
8 oz (225 g) large green pasta shells, cooked and well drained
8 oz (225 g) large white pasta shells, cooked and well drained
3 tomatoes, skinned and cut into strips
Chopped fresh parsley

Mix the cheese with the White Sauce while hot. Melt the butter and fry the mushrooms, adding the garlic when nearly cooked. Mix together the pasta, half the sauce and mushrooms with the pan juices and turn on to a heatproof dish. Scatter the raw tomato on top. Cover with the rest of the sauce and sprinkle with parsley. Reheat before serving.

SPICY BEAN AND SAUSAGE HOT-POT
Serves 6

4 oz (100 g) red kidney beans, dried or tinned
1 × 2 lb (900 g) tin Italian tomatoes
4 oz (100 g) haricot beans, dried or tinned
1 tablespoon tomato purée
1 × 7 oz (200 g) tin baked beans (optional)
4 oz (100 g) 'cocktail' pork sausages
4 oz (100 g) Polish boiling ring, sliced
2 tablespoons vegetable oil
2 oz (50 g) frozen baby onions or sliced onions
4 oz (100 g) fatty ham, cubed
1 clove garlic, crushed
2 shakes Tabasco sauce, or a good pinch
of Mexican chilli powder
Salt and freshly ground black pepper
Chopped fresh parsley

If using dried kidney and haricot beans, mix them with the tinned tomatoes and their liquid and soak overnight. If you're using dried kidney beans be very careful how you cook them. For further advice see Michael Barry's recipe for Rice and Peas (page 126). If using tinned beans, overnight soaking will not be necessary. Simmer until the beans are soft, adding water if necessary. When the beans are cooked, boil hard to evaporate most of the liquid. Then stir in the tomato purée and baked beans, if using. Fry the sausages and Polish ring in the oil, then the onions, then the ham and finally the garlic, adding them, as they are done, to the beans. Season with Tabasco sauce or chilli powder, salt and pepper. Freeze, or refrigerate for later, or dish up and eat. Garnish with parsley just before serving.

BROWN SUGAR MERINGUES
Makes 6

7 egg whites
4 oz (100 g) caster sugar
4 oz (100 g) soft brown sugar

For the filling
1 × 5 fl oz (150 ml) carton whipping cream
3 tablespoons lemon curd

Use an electric whisk to whisk together all the meringue ingredients, except 2 tablespoons caster sugar. Fold this in at the point when the mixture is too stiff to flow at all from a lifted whisk. Shape into 12 meringue shells on greased and floured foil. Bake at 275° F (140° C), gas mark 1, until crisp and dry right through.

To make the filling, whip the cream until stiff, then fold in the lemon curd. When the meringues are cool, sandwich pairs together with the filling.

APRICOT JALOUSIE

8 oz (225 g) dried apricots, soaked overnight
3 oz (75 g) sugar
1 oz (25 g) Demerara sugar
1 lb (450 g) puff pastry, thawed if frozen
1 egg, beaten
Icing sugar, to glaze (optional)

Drain the apricots, then stew with the sugars, until tender. Roll the pastry out very thinly, and cut into eight squares about 4 × 4 inches (10 × 10 cm). Divide the cooled apricots between four of the squares, leaving a margin. Wet the edges, cover with the remaining pastry, press to seal and cut slashes through the top pastry to allow the steam to escape. Brush with beaten egg and bake at 450°F (230°C), gas mark 8, for 18 minutes or until well browned.

For a shiny sugar glaze, dredge the finished jalousies heavily with icing sugar and brown under a very hot grill.

INDEX